DK EYEWITNESS TRAVEL

TOP 10
MALTA & GOZO

W9-AEG-095

WITHDRAWN
BY
WILLIAMSBURG REGIONAL LIBRARY

MARY-ANN GALLAGHER

Top 10 Malta and Gozo Highlights

The Top 10 of Everything

CONTENTS

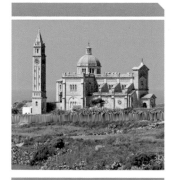

Malta and Gozo Area by Area

Streetsmart

**The information in this DK Eyewitness
Top 10 Travel Guide is checked regularly.**
Every effort has been made to ensure that
this book is as up-to-date as possible at
the time of going to press. Some details,
however, such as telephone numbers,
opening hours, prices, gallery hanging
arrangements and travel information, are
liable to change. The publishers cannot
accept responsibility for any consequences
arising from the use of this book, nor for any
material on third party websites, and cannot
guarantee that any website address in this
book will be a suitable source of travel
information. We value the views and
suggestions of our readers very highly.
Please write to: Publisher, DK Eyewitness
Travel Guides, Dorling Kindersley, 80 Strand,
London WC2R 0RL, Great Britain, or email
travelguides@dk.com

Within each Top 10 list in this book, no hierarchy
of quality or popularity is implied. All 10 are, in
the editor's opinion, of roughly equal merit.

Front cover and spine *Valletta skyline, pierced
by the dome of the Carmelite Church*
Back cover *The crystal blue waters of Għajn
Tuffieħa Bay, Northern Malta*
Title page *Traditional Luzzu fishing boat*

Welcome to
Malta and Gozo

Enclosed by the sparkling blue waters of the Mediterranean, the tiny nation of Malta packs an extraordinary amount into three compact, easily visited, islands – sight-rich Malta, restful Gozo and tiny Comino. The sun shines 300 days of the year and the sea is warm from early summer to well into autumn. But it isn't just about sun and sea: Malta boasts 7,000 years of history, culture and world-class architecture. With Eyewitness Top 10 Malta and Gozo, they are yours to explore.

Maltese sights range from unique, ancient stone temples, like **Mnajdra** and **Ħaġar Qim**, to iconic 21st-century structures at Valletta's **City Gate**. The nation's position at the heart of the Mediterranean and its vast natural harbours have attracted every power in the region. The Phoenicians came first, leaving their legacy in the form of Malta's traditional boats, seen in glorious technicolour in **Marsaxlokk Harbour**. The Romans, Arabs, medieval Christians, Ottoman Turks, French and British all left their mark, as did World War II and above all the Knights of Malta.

The Knights built Malta's delightful little capital, **Valletta**, its 16th-century bastion walls towering dramatically over the Grand Harbour and its narrow streets of honeyed limestone glowing in the Mediterranean sun. Many of the Knights' buildings have survived along with their art, including **St John's Co-Cathedral**, which features perhaps Europe's most dazzling Baroque interior.

Whether you're coming for a weekend or a week, our Top 10 guide brings together the best of everything Malta and Gozo have to offer, from castles and catacombs to culinary delectations. The guide gives you tips throughout, from seeking out what's free to avoiding the crowds, plus eight easy-to-follow itineraries, designed to help you visit a clutch of sights in a short space of time. Add inspiring photography and detailed maps, and you've got the essential pocket-sized travel companion. **Enjoy the book, and enjoy Malta and Gozo.**

Clockwise from top: **Blue Lagoon in Comino, Popeye Village in Anchor Bay, Valletta skyline with the dome of Carmelite Church, Mnajdra temple, decorative detail at St John's Co-Cathedral in Valletta, Għadira Nature Reserve, Mdina Citadel**

Exploring Malta and Gozo

Malta's reputation may be for sun and sea, but the islands are packed with historic and cultural sights. The distances to travel are short and there's good transport so you can fit a lot into a few days. Here are some ideas for two- and seven-day trips, focusing on the places that no one should miss.

Two Days in Malta

Day ❶

MORNING

Enter **Valletta** *(see pp64–71)* through **City Gate** *(see p68)* and walk down **Republic Street** *(see p68)* to **St John's Co-Cathedral** *(see pp14–17)*, one of Europe's most extravagant Baroque churches. Visit the **Grand Master's Palace** *(see pp12–13)* then grab some food before dropping into the **National Museum of Archaeology** *(see p65)*.

AFTERNOON

Hop on a bus (or drive) to **Mnajdra** and **Ħaġar Qim** *(see pp18–19)*, the best examples of Malta's unique Neolithic temples. Head on to **Rabat** *(see pp20–21)* to see the Roman cata-combs and **Mdina** *(see pp20–21)* – a perfect place to stroll as afternoon turns to evening and dinner time.

Valletta is a hub of ancient artifacts, many displayed in the Museum of Archaeology.

Day ❷

MORNING

Visit the prehistoric **Ħal Saflieni Hypogeum** *(see pp28–9)* and the neighbouring **Tarxien Temples** *(see p95)*. Head to **Marsaxlokk** *(see pp26–7)* for a fish lunch on the harbour.

AFTERNOON

Explore the deeply historic streets of **Birgu** *(see pp24–5)* before taking the Three Cities ferry across the Grand Harbour and the lift up to the **Upper Barrakka Gardens** *(see p58)*. Enjoy panoramic views before wandering into Valletta for supper.

Seven Days in Malta and Gozo

Day ❶

Spend the morning as per day one of the two-day itinerary. Take your time in the **National Museum of Archaeology** *(see p65)* and then

St John's Co-Cathedral has a dazzling interior and holds many treasures.

One of the best views of Birgu is from Valletta looking back across the Grand Harbour.

Key

— Two-day itinerary
— Seven-day itinerary

Day ❸
Be first at Malta's unique **Mnajdra** and **Ħaġar Qim** temples *(see pp18–19)*. Go on to **Marsaxlokk** *(see pp26–7)* for a fish lunch on the harbour. Take in the extraordinary **Ħal Saflieni Hypogeum** *(see pp28–9)* and the nearby **Tarxien Temples** *(see p95)*.

Day ❹
Stroll through **Mdina** *(see pp20–21)* taking in the cathedral and museums before walking into **Rabat** *(see pp20–21)* to visit the Roman catacombs. Stop off at **Mosta Dome** *(see p90–91)*.

Day ❺
Take a tour of **Palazzo Parisio** *(see p89)* and drop by the Red Tower at **Marfa Ridge** *(see p82)* en route to the Gozo ferry *(see p108)*. Once on Gozo, enjoy a Gozitan lunch at **Ta' Rikardu** *(see p105)* before taking a walk around the **Citadel** *(see pp30–31)*. Head to the gorgeous red sands at **Ramla Bay** *(see p103)* to relax and swim. Stay over on Gozo for a couple of nights.

Day ❻
Take a boat trip around the coast and over to **Comino** *(see pp34–5)* where you can swim and snorkel in the beguiling Blue Lagoon.

Day ❼
During your last day on Gozo, visit **Dwejra** *(see pp32–3)* before heading to the ferry to return to Malta.

Fungus Rock is a notable landmark in Dwejra Bay off Gozo.

visit **St Paul's Shipwreck Church** *(see p66)* and **Manoel Theatre** *(see p66)* before deciding on a restaurant for a leisurely Valletta dinner.

Day ❷
Take some time to wander the narrow streets of **Valletta** *(see pp64–71)* and its towering fortifications, such as Fort St Elmo and the **National War Museum** *(see p40)*. Fully appreciate the panoramic views from the **Upper Barrakka Gardens** *(see p58)* before taking the lift down to the Three Cities ferry and crossing the Grand Harbour to explore the medieval town of **Birgu** *(see pp24–5)*.

Top 10 Malta and Gozo Highlights

Colourful fishing boats in the pretty harbour at Marsaxlokk

⏀ Malta and Gozo Highlights

The tiny Maltese archipelago, floating on the cusp of Europe and Africa, has been coveted and invaded throughout its history – the Knights of St John, the British, and the islands' earliest settlers have all made their mark on Malta. The largest island has the most cosmopolitan resorts and cultural treasures, while unspoiled Gozo and tiny Comino offer a gentler pace of life.

① Grand Master's Palace, Valletta

This is a fittingly splendid home for the supreme head of the Knights. The opulent rooms are filled with treasures ranging from paintings to elaborate friezes (see pp12–13).

② St John's Co-Cathedral, Valletta

This, one of the world's finest Baroque churches, still belongs to the Knights of Malta. The Oratory contains Caravaggio's masterpiece, *The Beheading of St John the Baptist* (see pp14–17).

③ Mnajdra and Ħaġar Qim Temples

These beautiful temples made of creamy limestone are set on a wild and rugged clifftop overlooking the sea (see pp18–19).

④ Mdina and Rabat

Malta's ancient capital Mdina is a magical city girdled by sturdy walls and full of fine palaces and churches. Rabat, next door, has some of the most important Christian sites in Malta (see pp20–21).

⑤ Birgu (Vittoriosa)

Charming Birgu, with its narrow medieval streets criss-crossing a peninsula in the Grand Harbour, was the Knights first base in Malta, with Fort St Angelo as their military headquarters (see pp24–5).

6 Marsaxlokk

In this enchanting little fishing village, brightly painted *luzzus* (boats) bob in the bay. Maltese families pour in on Sundays to visit the fish market on the quays, and then to linger in the seafront restaurants *(see pp26–7)*.

7 Ħal Saflieni Hypogeum, Paola

Over 55 centuries ago, men hewed this necropolis out of solid rock. The chambers, spread over three levels, are magnificently carved and decorated *(see pp28–9)*.

8 The Citadel, Victoria, Gozo

The tiny walled Citadel sits high on a lofty promontory in the centre of Gozo; from here, views unfold across the island and beyond to Malta. Within its walls are fascinating museums *(see pp30–31)*.

Mellieħa
St Paul's Bay
Bugibba
Mediterranean Sea
Qadi
Dragu
Paceville
Mġarr
Naxxar
St Julian's
Sliema
Mosta
Gżira
Birkirkara
Valletta
Attard
Ħamrun
Birgu
Mdina and Rabat
Qormi
Żebbuġ
Żabbar
Ħal Saflieni Hypogeum
Marsaskala
Dingli
Ta' Brija
Siġġiewi
Tarxien
Żejtun
Gudja
Malta
Kirkop
Marsaxlokk
Qrendi
Mnajdra and Ħaġar Qim
Żurrieq
Ta' Għammur
Birżebbuġa

0 kilometres 4
0 miles 4

9 Dwejra, Gozo

Gozo's western coastline is spectacular around Dwejra, where dramatic rock formations frame stunning views of the receding cliffs. It's perfect hiking territory, and the diving is among the best in the Mediterranean *(see pp32–3)*.

10 Comino

The smallest island in the Maltese archipelago, tiny Comino is an unspoiled wilderness with a minuscule population. You can swim in azure waters at the Blue Lagoon or hike to spectacular cliffs *(see pp34–5)*.

TOP 10 ⭐ Grand Master's Palace, Valletta

This handsome palace was built between 1573 and 1578 by the celebrated Maltese architect Gerolamo Cassar (1520–86). Today it is the office of the president, but for over 200 years it was home to the Grand Master, supreme head of the Order of the Knights of St John. Here, the Grand Master would greet foreign envoys and important guests, and the State Apartments are suitably crammed with reminders of the Order's fabulous wealth and influence.

5 Tapestry Chamber

In this elegant room, the Knights attended to day-to-day business and, in later years, the Maltese parliament. It is dimly lit to preserve the sumptuous Gobelin tapestries.

6 Great Siege Frieze

This dynamic frieze **(below)** recounting the key events in the Knights' celebrated defence of the island was painted between 1575 and 1581 by Matteo Perez d'Aleccio.

1 Ambassador's Room

The Grand Masters used this chamber **(above)** for private audiences and to meet foreign dignitaries. Lionello Spada painted the frieze, which shows moments in the history of the Order of St John.

THE MALTESE CROSS

The eight-pointed cross is the symbol of the Knights of Malta. Its eight points symbolize the Beatitudes and the original *Langues* (national "tongues") of the Order. The four arms are supposed to represent the four cardinal Virtues: Fortitude, Justice, Temperance and Perseverance. Although said to date back to the founding of the Order in the 11th century, this style of cross came into common use only in the the mid-16th century.

2 State Dining Hall

Damaged by bombing during World War II, this beautiful chamber is lined with portraits of a British monarch and Maltese heads of state.

3 Neptune's Courtyard

The statue **(left)** that gives its name to the courtyard is attributed to Flemish sculptor Giambologna (1529–1608). It is said that Admiral Andrea Doria, a friend of Grand Master de Vallette, posed for it.

4 Gobelin Tapestries

Known as *Les Tentures des Indes* (the Indies Tapestries), for their depictions of exotic scenes, these tapestries were donated in 1710 by Grand Master Perellos.

8 Corridors of the Knights

On the first floor of the palace, lavishly decorated marble corridors **(left)** overlook Neptune's Courtyard. Portraits of the Grand Masters, their coats of arms and suits of armour are displayed.

9 Armoury

The Palace Armoury, located in the former stables, contains more than 5,000 pieces of military hardware. These include a bronze cannon, firearms and suits of armour originally used by 16th- and 17th-century troops in battle.

10 Parade Armour

The highlight of this collection is the parade armour **(below)** made for the Grand Masters. The suit made for Grand Master Alof de Wignacourt (1601–22) has gold and silver inlaid patterns.

7 Supreme Council Hall

This grand room has chandeliers and a frieze of paintings depicting the Great Siege of 1565. The minstrel's gallery at one end once decorated the palace chapel, but came originally from the warship *Grand Carrack* in which the Knights travelled from Rhodes to Malta.

NEED TO KNOW

MAP J2 ▪ Triq Ir-Repubblika ▪ 2124 9349 ▪ www.heritagemalta.org (armoury and state rooms)

Open palace 10am–4pm Fri–Wed; armoury 9am–5pm daily

Adm palace and armoury: €10, concessions €7, under-11s €5; audio-guide free with admission ticket

▪ The palace may be closed for official presidential duties; check with the tourist office in advance. If it is closed, the entrance price for just the armoury will be €6, concessions €4.50, under 11s €3.

▪ There are lots of cafés in the vicinity. The wine bar Ambrosia *(see p71)* serves delicious light meals.

TOP 10 ★ St John's Co-Cathedral, Valletta

Designed by Gerolamo Cassar and consecrated in 1578, St John's looms over Valletta like a giant fortress. Yet when you step over the threshold, the austerity gives way to dazzling beauty and treasures. The marble floor is covered with richly inlaid tombstones, every wall is intricately carved with flowers and garlands, and the vaulted ceiling is splendidly painted with frescoes by Mattia Preti (1613–99).

1 Nave
The nave **(above)** was at first as plain as the façade. It was changed in the 1660s, when Preti gave it a Baroque makeover and painted his frescoes of episodes from the life of St John.

2 Façade
The cathedral's unadorned façade **(below)** reflects its role as the centrepiece of the new fortress-city.

St John's Co-Cathedral

3 Chapel of Our Lady of Philermos
This chapel housed the icon of the Virgin of Philermos brought from Rhodes, though today it houses the Virgin of Lanciano, also known as the Virgin of Carafa.

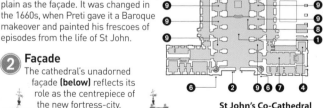

5 Marble Tombstones

The floor of the church is a sea of marble, where 400 Knights are buried under dazzling tombstones. Each is adorned with the coat of arms of its aristocratic occupant, along with symbols that are a reminder of the inevitability of death **(left)**

6 Bell Towers

The severe bell towers flanking the main entrance are the model for the twin bell towers that adorn virtually every church in Malta.

7 Oratory

The Oratory boasts Caravaggio's masterpiece and Malta's most famous artwork, *The Beheading of St John the Baptist* (1608).

8 Monument of Grand Master Cotoner

The bronze bust of the diplomat and strategist is carried by two slaves, who represent Asia and Africa.

9 Chapels of the Langues

Each of the *Langues* (the national chapters of the Order of St John) was given its own chapel off one of the aisles on either side of the nave **(right)**. The *Langues* vied with each other to create the most lavish chapel.

CARAVAGGIO

When celebrated painter Caravaggio (1571–1610) arrived on Malta in 1607, he had a price on his head for killing a man in a brawl. In spite of this, he impressed the Grand Master and was made a Knight. But soon after painting *The Beheading of St John the Baptist* in 1608 he was imprisoned for injuring another Knight. He escaped, but was stripped of his Knighthood as a "foul and rotten member".

10 High Altar

The 17th-century High Altar is made of gold, silver and bronze, and encrusted with jewels in many hues *(see p16)*.

4 Museum

The museum displays treasures of the Knights, including important Grand Master paintings, lavishly embroidered vestments, illuminated antiphonaries, silver plates and a fine collection of 17th-century tapestries, designed by Rubens *(see p40)*.

NEED TO KNOW

MAP H2/J2 ■ Misraħ San Ġwann (visitors' entrance on Triq Ir-Repubblika) ■ 2122 0536 ■ www.stjohnscocathedral.org

Open 9:30am–4pm Mon–Fri, 9:30am–noon Sat

Adm €10, seniors & students €7.50, under-12s free

■ The museum has recently been refurbished – check ahead for possible closures

■ You may be refused entry if you are not dressed respectfully. Shoes with high heels are not allowed as they can damage the floor, but you can buy protective slippers for €1.

■ Nearby Caffe Cordina *(see p70)* has tables out on the square.

Treasures of St John's Co-Cathedral

Caravaggio's *The Beheading of St John the Baptist*

1 The Beheading of St John the Baptist (1608)
Caravaggio's emotive masterpiece depicts the moment after the sword has dropped and St John the Baptist has fallen, bleeding, to the ground.

2 Grim Reaper Memorial Stone
Entering the cathedral, you can't miss the depiction of the Grim Reaper, scythe aloft, which adorns the tombstone of a French Knight. The inscription reads "You who tread on me will soon be trodden on".

3 Altarpiece of St George
The altarpiece in the Chapel of Aragon was originally Mattia Preti's calling card – he sent it to Malta as an example of his work. It led to his commission to paint the church's ceiling frescoes.

4 Embroidered Vestments
The Cathedral Museum contains ornate robes from the 16th century. Most belonged to the Spanish Grand Master Nicolas Cotoner.

5 Monstrance
This Baroque monstrance was made to hold the reliquary containing the right hand of St John the Baptist. Stolen by Napoleon, the reliquary was lost at sea.

6 Portraits of the Grand Masters
A series of portraits by the French artist Antoine de Favray (1706–c.1791) are highlights of the painting gallery. The best is his depiction of the pleasure-loving Grand Master Pinto de Fonseca.

7 Tombs of the Grand Masters
The resplendent Chapels of the Langues contain monuments to the Grand Masters. One of the most lavish belongs to Grand Master Ramón Perellos in the Chapel of Aragon.

8 Tapestries
Flemish tapestries, based on cartoons by Rubens and Poussin, are among the most precious objects in the Cathedral Museum.

9 Blessed Sacrament Gate
It is said this silver gate was painted black to foil Napoleon's rapacious troops. It is one of the few silver objects to survive the plunder.

10 High Altar
The High Altar (1686) is a flamboyant Baroque design in gilded silver, studded with precious jewels. At the centre, a relief in gilded bronze depicts the Last Supper.

The High Altar, encrusted with jewels

THE KNIGHTS OF ST JOHN

Tower of St Nicolas in the Siege of Rhodes

The Order of the Knights of St John was founded in Jerusalem in the 11th century and is the oldest Order of Chivalry in existence. The Knights were required to show proof of noble birth (an ancient rule that was only modified in the 1990s) and were organized into national chapters called *Langues*. The supreme head is the Grand Master. After the fall of Jerusalem in the late 13th century, the Knights built an island fortress on Rhodes. In 1480, Grand Master Pierre d'Aubusson successfully defended Rhodes against an Ottoman siege. The Knights were, however, ousted by the Ottomans in 1522. The Holy Roman Emperor Charles V offered the Knights the Maltese islands in exchange for the annual payment of a live Maltese falcon, and they arrived in Malta in 1530. They withstood the Turks during the Great Siege of 1565, built the walled city of Valletta and erected defences across the islands. In the 17th and 18th centuries, as the Ottoman threat diminished, the Order fell into decline. When Napoleon arrived on Maltese shores in 1798, the Knights submitted to the French without a fight. They were forced to leave Malta, but the Order refused to be crushed. Although still stateless today, it continues to exist, focusing primarily on charitable and religious works.

TOP 10
IMPORTANT DATES FOR THE KNIGHTS OF ST JOHN

1 c.1100: The Order is founded after First Crusade.

2 1279: The Knights leave Jerusalem as the Muslims take control.

3 1309: The Knights take the island of Rhodes.

4 1522: The Ottomans oust the Knights from Rhodes.

5 1530: The Knights are given Malta by Charles V.

6 1565: The Knights claim victory over the Ottomans in the first Great Siege.

7 1571: The Ottomans are defeated at the Battle of Lepanto.

8 1660s: Mattia Preti transforms St John's into a Baroque masterpiece.

9 1792: Revolutionaries seize the Order of the Knight's considerable French assets.

10 1798: The Knights cede Malta to Napoleon.

Gun-wielding Ottomans attacked the Knights of St John during the siege of Rhodes in 1480.

TOP 10 ⭐ Mnajdra and Ħaġar Qim Temples

These ancient limestone temples, built between 3600 and 2500 BC (before even the famous circle at Stonehenge), are the best preserved and most evocative of Malta's unique UNESCO World Heritage Megalithic temples. They are located in an attractive rural landscape, where relatively little has changed since the temple period; their monumental doorways, internal rooms, steps and altars bear astonishing witness to the craftsmanship of the people of these islands 5,000 years ago. There are three quite typical temples at Mnajdra, while Ħaġar Qim, on a limestone acropolis, is unusual and home to some of Malta's most intriguing early carvings.

NEED TO KNOW

MAP C6 ■ Triq Ħaġar Qim, beyond Qrendi
■ 2142 4231 ■ www.heritagemalta.org

Open 9am–5:30pm daily (to 4:30pm in winter)

Adm €10, concessions €7.50, children €5.50

■ Special early morning tours are organized by Heritage Malta four times a year (on the solstices and equinoxes) to see the first rays of the rising sun hit certain stones. Make sure you book early as there's a very long waiting list.

■ Toilets are in the visitor centre, close to the entrance to Ħaġar Qim.

1 External Altar, Ħaġar Qim

Just beyond the gigantic stone is an exterior shrine **(above)** and elliptical hole. At sunrise on the first day of summer, also known as the summer solstice, the sun's rays pass through the hole forming a crescent on one of the megaliths inside.

2 Main Entrance, Ħaġar Qim

Ħaġar Qim's dramatic main entrance **(below)** remains surprisingly intact, with its large honey-coloured stones neatly interlocking.

3 Gigantic Stone, Ħaġar Qim

The biggest stone in the complex is to the right of the main entrance. It measures a huge 21 sq m (220 sq ft) and weighs 20 tons.

4 Decorative Objects, Ħaġar Qim

The most notable objects found at Ħaġar Qim are statuettes. It is famous for this figure (right) of a female, popularly known as the "Venus of Malta".

6 Carved Doorway, South Temple, Mnajdra

This carved doorway is one of the best pieces of original stonework still in situ in Malta's temples. It is framed by three stones featuring pitted designs.

A STONE CALENDAR

Mnajdra's South Temple displays an extraordinary astronomical alignment. At the equinoxes, which take place on 21 March and 23 September, the sunlight shines through the main doorway. At the summer solstice on 21 June, the rays fall on the large stone to the left of the doorway, while at the winter solstice on 22 December, they fall on the corresponding right-hand stone.

7 Small Temple, Mnajdra

Almost nothing survives of the smallest temple in Mnajdra (below), which dates from the Ġgantija era. One of the oldest free-standing monuments, it has pitted decorations that may tally the rising of particular constellations.

10 Islet of Filfla

This tiny, mostly barren, offshore islet is now a wildlife reserve, but it retains its ancient mystique. It is thought that it may have had special significance for the temple-builders.

5 Misqa Tanks

A trail leading off the main passage takes you to a hill pocked with bell-shaped water tanks, probably carved out of the rock in order to collect rainwater and provide the temples with water.

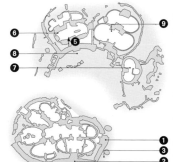

Mnajdra and Ħaġar Qim Temples

8 Façade of South Temple, Mnajdra

The South Temple is one of the best preserved in all Malta. The façade has a long exterior bench; outdoor rituals may have taken place in the front courtyard.

9 Carving of Temple Façade, Central Temple, Mnajdra

The most recent of the three, the Central Temple was built between the two existing temples. One of its huge orthostats shows a carved representation of a temple façade – perhaps an early architectural design.

TOP 10 ★ Mdina and Rabat

Mdina is Malta's most hauntingly beautiful city – a medieval citadel on Arab and Roman foundations. This was Malta's capital until the construction of Valletta and remained the favoured home of its aristocratic families, who still own palaces here. Mdina remains a tiny time capsule of a city, while Rabat, the town just outside the Mdina bastions, is more of a modern workaday town. Nonetheless, Rabat boasts some important Christian sights, from the cave where St Paul is said to have lived to early Christian catacombs.

ST AGATHA

St Paul is Malta's most important saint, but St Agatha comes a close second. According to legend, the beautiful young virgin Agatha, a native of Sicily, caught the eye of the Roman governor but refused his advances. She fled to Malta to escape from persecution. The saint is said to have prayed in a small cave in Rabat, and an underground chapel was later built there in her memory. After a while she returned to Sicily and was then captured by the Roman governor, who had her tortured and killed.

2 Palazzo Vilhena, Mdina

Grand Master Vilhena commissioned Guion de Mondion to build this Baroque palace (**above**) in 1726. Most of its opulence was stripped when it became a hospital. It now houses the Natural History Museum.

3 Palazzo Falzon, Mdina

Several collections, from silver and jewellery to Persian rugs, fill this palace, one of the oldest houses in the city.

4 Walls and Gates, Mdina

The imposing city walls were first built by the Arabs. The lavish Baroque main gate was built in 1724 and later restored. The beautiful gardens below enhance the visual appeal of the area.

1 St Paul's Cathedral, Mdina

Lorenzo Gafa's handsome Baroque cathedral (**below**) is topped by an elegant dome. The marble tombstones laid into the floor are dedicated to notable prelates.

9 St Agatha in the Catacombs, Rabat

St Agatha is said to have prayed in these subterranean tombs. The main chapel is decorated with beautiful medieval frescoes **(left)**. Half-lost within the catacombs is another exquisitely painted chapel from the 4th century AD.

5 Triq Villegaignon, Mdina

Mdina's main street is lined with the city's oldest and most beautiful palaces, many occupied by noble families prominent in Malta to this day. The decorative doorknockers are particularly delightful.

10 Domvs Romana, Rabat

On the outskirts of Rabat, near Mdina's Greek Gate, this complex consists of a small museum and the time-worn ruins of an opulent Roman town house. The museum contains some wonderful mosaics and sculptures.

Mdina and Rabat

St Paul's Church and Grotto, Rabat 6

St Paul **(right)** is said to have lived in this grotto during his stay in Malta, and the cave remains a place of pilgrimage. The church itself is gloomy, but it contains a statue of the Madonna said to have miraculous powers.

7 Cathedral Museum, Mdina

Housed in a faded Baroque building with a marble staircase, this museum is quirky and old-fashioned. The highlight is a series of Dürer woodcuts.

8 St Paul's Catacombs, Rabat

These fascinating Phoenician catacombs, a handful of which have their original decoration, were also used by early Christians.

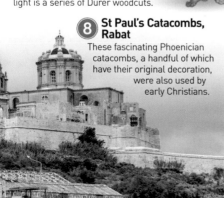

NEED TO KNOW
MAP C4

St Paul's Cathedral, Mdina: Pjazza San Pawl; 2145 4697; open 9:30am–4pm Mon–Fri (to 3pm Sat)

Palazzo Vilhena, Mdina: Pjazza San Publiju; 2145 5951; open 9am–4:30pm daily; adm €5

Palazzo Falzon, Mdina: Triq Villegaignon; 2145 4512; open 10am–4pm Tue–Sun; adm €10

St Paul's Church and Grotto, Rabat: Misraħ Il-Paroċċa; 2145 4467; open 9am–5pm Mon–Sat

Cathedral Museum, Mdina: Pjazza ta' l-Arcisqof; 2145 4697; open 9:30am–4pm Mon–Fri (to 3pm Sat); adm €5

St Paul's (St Agatha's) Catacombs, Rabat: Triq Sant' Agata; 2145 4526; open 9am–4:30 daily; adm €4

Domvs Romana, Rabat: Il-Wesgħa Tal-Mużew; 2145 4125; open 9am–4:30pm daily; adm €6, children €3

■ St Paul's Catacombs offers an audio-guide.

TOP 10 ★ Birgu (Vittoriosa)

On the banks of the Grand Harbour opposite Valletta stand the Three Cities, the most historic of which is Birgu. A medieval harbour town, it became the Knights' first base in Malta in 1530. It was from here that the Knights held out against the besieging Ottoman Turks in the Great Siege of 1565, earning the town its official name of Vittoriosa. Abandoned for Valletta in 1571, Birgu became a quiet backwater until the arrival of the Royal Navy, which was based here throughout the 19th century and during World War II until the last troops left the city in 1979.

1 Vittoriosa Waterfront
Once the Knights treasury and wharf, this area is now a yacht marina **(above)**. A row of pleasant waterfront restaurants and cafés between Fort St Angelo and the rest of Birgu are perfect for lunch.

Birgu (Vittoriosa)

2 Inquisitor's Palace
Home of the Inquisition in Malta for over 220 years, this medieval house still has cells, a tribunal room and a torture chamber. It also houses the Museum of Ethnography.

3 Church of St Lawrence
This was the Knights first church in Malta where they gathered before and after the Great Siege. Today's structure **(left)** was designed by Lorenzo Gafa in the 16th century.

4 The Collachio
This atmospheric maze of medieval streets is where the Knights had their first homes in Malta – there is one auberge for each language group (all are closed to the public).

Previous pages The Crystal Lagoon on the island of Comino

6 Auberge d'Angleterre

This is the only English auberge **(left)** in Malta. When the Knights came to Valletta the Reformation had put an end to the English role in the Order.

7 Oratory Museum

The little museum of the Church of St Lawrence houses the hat and sword used by Grand Master Jean de Valette during the Great Siege of 1565.

8 Dock No. 1

This was the Grand Harbour home of the British Royal Navy ships in the Mediterranean. Now restored, it makes a pleasant waterside walk.

BAND CLUBS

In Birgu's main square is the St Lawrence Band Club, identified by its filigree of white iron-work. Known in British times as the Duke of Edinburgh Band Club, it harks back to when military music wafted over these islands. Today each parish in Malta has a band, providing music for the annual *festa*.

10 Malta Maritime Museum

Originally the Royal Navy bakery, the museum houses models of ships that plied these creeks under the Knights and the British, as well as a 4-ton Roman anchor.

5 Malta at War Museum

More than a museum about World War II, this site includes a tour of one of the largest rock-cut bomb shelters in Malta.

9 Fort St Angelo

Malta's oldest fortress **(above)** traces its history from medieval times through the Knights' Great Siege to World War II, when it was HQ of the Royal Navy.

NEED TO KNOW

Inquisitor's Palace: **MAP L5**; Triq Il-Palazz Ta' L-Isqof; 2182 7006; open 9am–4:30pm daily; adm €6, youth (12–17) and concessions €4.50, children €3.00, under-5s free

Church of St Lawrence: **MAP L5**; Triq San Lawrenz; 2182 7057; open 7am–6pm daily

Malta at War Museum: **MAP L6**; Couvre Porte Gate; 2189 6617; open 10am–5pm daily; adm adult €12, concessions €10, children €5, family (2 adults, 3 children) €25

Auberge d'Angleterre: **MAP L5**; Majjistral

Fort St Angelo: **MAP K4**; 2540 1800; open 9am–5:30pm daily, closed bank hols; adm adult €8, youth (12–17) and concessions €5, children €3, under-5s free

Malta Maritime Museum: **MAP K5**; Vittoriosa Waterfront; 2166 0052; open 9am–4:30pm daily; adm adult €5, youth (12–17) and concessions €3.50, children €2.50, under-5s free

■ Catch the Three Cities ferry to cross the Grand Harbour between Valletta's Customs House and Birgu.

■ The best way to explore the area is on foot but to tour further afield you can hire a talking golf buggy from Rolling Geeks (*www.rolling-geeks.com*). You'll require a driving licence.

TOP 10 ⭐ Marsaxlokk

This enchanting fishing village is set around an azure bay. Traditional fishing boats painted in bright colours bob in the harbour, and the quays are spread with brilliantly coloured fishing nets. Life continues much as it has for decades in this small and tight-knit community, which has survived the daily deluge of tourists without selling its soul. The modern era has left some ugly marks: the power station out on Delimara Point blights the view, as does the container port around the headland. For now at least, Marsaxlokk's charms remain intact.

1 Quays

The picturesque harbour of Marsaxlokk is hemmed in by quays strewn with brilliantly coloured fishing nets of cobalt blue and emerald green. The local fishermen are usually hard at work fixing boats or mending nets **(below)**.

2 Luzzus

These traditional brightly painted boats **(above)** are said to owe their design to the ancient Phoenicians, who first arrived in Malta around 800 BC. The Eye of Osiris, an ancient symbol of protection against evil, is still painted on every prow.

3 Church of Our Lady of Pompeii

This pretty little church **(right)** sits just back from the harbour. As in many Maltese churches, it has two clocks – one painted and permanently set at a few moments before the witching hour of midnight to ward off evil spirits. The church also has some fine artworks.

NEED TO KNOW

MAP F5

Tourist Office: Xatt Is-Sajjieda; 2165 1151; open 9am–5:45pm Mon–Sat, 9am–12:45pm Sun & hols

■ Book early for Sunday lunch, as many Maltese families get together here for long meals.

■ There are numerous dining options all along the seafront. Try Ir-Rizzu *(see p99)*.

⑥ St Lucian's Tower

This squat little fortress **(above)** guards the headland beyond Marsaxlokk. It was erected by the Knights in 1610 as part of their coastal defences.

⑦ St Peter's Pool

Located close to Marsaxlokk, this swimming hole **(below)** is hidden away on the eastern side of Delimara Point. It's in an isolated spot so can be dangerous to swim if the waters are choppy.

⑨ Fish Restaurants

Several of the former fishermen's houses that surround the quays have been converted into fish restaurants. A long, lazy seafood lunch after a visit to the fish market is a Sunday tradition.

④ Sunday Fish Market

Marsaxlokk's fish market is a local legend. Locals and tourists alike come to gawp at the array of fabulous fresh produce on the seafront stalls. If buying fish, look for bright eyes and red gills.

⑤ Daily Market

A section of the Marsaxlokk quays is set aside for a popular daily market, where all kinds of items are sold, such as clothes, souvenirs, CDs and sunglasses. On Sundays, the tourist tat makes way for fresh fish.

⑧ Delimara Point

This long finger of land protrudes into the sea southeast of Marsaxlokk harbour. It is peaceful and rural, with tiny bays, fields, and wonderful walking opportunities – but the views are spoiled by a huge power plant.

⑩ "Seasick Summit" Monument

A monument on the coast road from Marsaxlokk to Birżebbuġa commemorates the meeting of Gorbachev and George Bush Sr on board a cruiser; this marked the end of the Cold War.

TOP 10 ⭐ Ħal Saflieni Hypogeum, Paola

This vast underground necropolis is one of the most extraordinary archaeological sites in the world. The upper level dates back to about 3600 BC, and two more levels were subsequently dug below. The stunning chambers echo the forms of the above-ground temples found across the islands. The red ochre paintings found at the site are the oldest and only prehistoric paintings found on the Maltese Islands.

5 Holy of Holies

This is the most impressive of all the chambers **(left)**, entered through a magnificent monumental façade, featuring a trilithon doorway carved into the rock.

6 Sleeping Lady

One of Malta's most beautiful ancient statues **(below)** depicts an enormously plump woman sleeping serenely. Perhaps she symbolizes death – or is it a priestess in a trance? The original statue is in the National Museum of Archaeology *(see p65)*.

1 Entrance Trilithon

Some constructions in the upper level were destroyed in the early 1900s. But some features, including a trilithon comprising two large stones supporting a lintel, have survived intact.

2 Upper Level

The upper level (3600–3300 BC) is the oldest section, and it is apparent that the temple-builders originally enlarged a natural cave. Ancient bones have been left in situ here.

3 Middle Level

The most important chambers – and the most accomplished examples of stone-carving and decoration – are found on this level (3000–2500 BC).

4 Lower Level

The lower level (3000–2500 BC) of the Hypogeum is reached via uneven steps. These lead to chambers separated by walls about 2 m (6 ft) in height, making movement from one room to the next difficult. This level was probably used for storage.

NEED TO KNOW

MAP E5 ◼ Triq Ic-Ċimiterju ◼ 2180 5019 ◼ www.heritagemalta.com

Open 9am–4pm daily

Adm €30, concessions €15, children €12, under-6s free; advance booking essential

◼ Book weeks in advance as only 80 people are allowed to visit the Hypogeum daily and there is a long waiting list.

◼ Photography is not allowed at the Hypogeum.

◼ An audio-guide leads visitors around the site, but staff are on hand if you need any assistance.

◼ It's a 10-minute walk from the Tarzien Temples to the Hypogeum.

8 Main Chamber

A fascinating series of recesses are carved into the roughly circular walls of the main chamber **(left)**. Their function still remains unclear, but perhaps statues were placed here, or perhaps the dead were left here before finally being laid to rest elsewhere.

THE HYPOGEUM AND THE XAGĦRA CIRCLE

The Hypogeum was first excavated in the early 1900s using rudimentary techniques, and most of the early notes were subsequently lost. The absence of information from the opening of this site was a huge blow to archaeologists, but the discovery of the Xagħra Circle in Gozo has given them fresh hope. The Xagħra Circle has been excavated, and the new information provided has improved understanding of the Hypogeum.

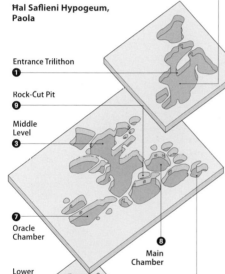

Ħal Saflieni Hypogeum, Paola

Upper Level **2**

Entrance Trilithon **1**

Rock-Cut Pit **9**

Middle Level **3**

Oracle Chamber **7**

Main Chamber **8**

Holy of Holies **5**

Lower Level **4**

Key to Floorplan
- ☐ Lower level
- ☐ Middle level
- ☐ Upper level

9 Rock-Cut Pit

Located just off the main chamber is a small cavern that is sometimes known as the "snake pit" or "votive pit". It has been suggested that the area was used for holding animals before they were sacrificed. The famous statue of the "Sleeping Lady" was found here.

10 Recovered Artifacts

The many artifacts found in the Hypogeum include amulets, figurines and vases. One of the most curious is a headless statue. It was found with two limestone heads, one of which fits perfectly.

7 Oracle Chamber

Ochre swirls decorate the ceiling **(right)** of this amazing chamber. A niche carved into the wall can be used to great theatrical effect; it allows low-pitched voices to reverberate impressively around the chamber.

TOP10 ⭐ The Citadel, Victoria, Gozo

All roads in Gozo lead to Victoria. The Gozitan capital is crowned by the walled Citadel, whose handsome silhouette is visible from almost everywhere on the island. For many years, the island of Gozo was plagued by raiding corsairs, Saracens and Turks, who took the people into slavery. Life was so risky that right up until 1673 the population was required by law to spend every night within the Citadel. Fresh from restoration, the improved Citadel is more accessible and offers magnificent views, a fine cathedral and a couple of museums.

1 Late Medieval Ruins

Much of the northern part of the Citadel **(right)** consists of ruined houses, walls and streets, which in many cases have been reduced to rubble. Many of these date back to the 15th century; EU funds are being sought to enable reconstruction.

2 Walls

The sturdy walls of the Citadel owe their solid appearance to the Knights, who had them substantially reinforced after their victory over the Turks in 1565. Although the Turkish threat had been quelled, the Knights feared vengeance.

3 Gran Castello Historic House (Folklore Museum)

A clutch of the oldest houses in the Citadel have been connected to form this museum. Displays of rural life include a reconstruction of a home, a grain mill **(left)** and tools for various crafts.

4 Gunpowder Magazine, Battery, WWII Shelter and Silos

At this site you can visit what was the Knights' first specialist gunpowder store, the inside of the Knights' grain store silos and a World War II shelter with a secret tunnel.

5 Cathedral

The lavish Baroque cathedral **(above)** was designed by Lorenzo Gafa and completed in 1716. A Roman temple to Juno is believed to have occupied the site a couple of thousand years ago.

The Citadel (Victoria), Gozo

7 City Gate

The Citadel has two gates: the restored original and one punched through the walls in 1956 to allow the cathedral's *festa* statue to pass through.

8 Museum of Archaeology

This museum contains artifacts from Ġgantija, Xagħra Circle and other Gozitan sites. Look out for the notable "shaman's bundle" **(below)**.

6 Cathedral Museum

The Cathedral Museum contains some quirky items, including the stole of El Salvadorean Archbishop Oscar Romero, assassinated in 1980 while saying Mass.

DRAGUT RAIS AND THE RAID OF 1551

Gozo, hard to defend, suffered countless raids by pirates and corsairs. The worst was in 1551, when corsair Dragut Rais attacked the Citadel and took nearly 6,000 people into slavery – virtually the entire population. A local soldier, Bernardo DeOpuo, could not bear the idea of his family being enslaved so he slit their throats rather than allow their capture. A street in the Citadel is named after him.

9 Old Prison

In use from the mid-16th to the 20th centuries, the cells and corridors are etched with prisoners' graffiti, such as a rendition of a galley with its oars. As a young man, Grand Master de la Valette was imprisoned here after a brawl.

10 Gozo Nature Museum

This museum, located in a 17th-century inn, has exhibits on Gozo's wildlife, geography and geology. Pride of place goes to four pieces of moon rock, donated to Malta by the US President Richard Nixon.

NEED TO KNOW

MAP D2

Gran Castello Historic House: Triq Bernardo DeOpuo; 2156 2034; open daily; adm €5 (combined ticket)

Gunpowder Magazine, Battery, WWII Shelter and Silos: Triq il-Foss; 2291 5452; open Mon–Fri

Cathedral: Pjazza Katidral; 2155 4101; open Mon–Sat

Cathedral Museum: Triq il-Foss; 2155 6087; open daily; adm €5.50

Gozo Nature Museum: Triq Il-Kwartier San Martin; 2155 6153; open daily

Old Prison: Pjazza Katidral; 2156 5988; open daily

Museum of Archaeology: Triq Bieb L-Imdina; 2155 6144; open daily; adm €5 (combined ticket)

■ Audio-guides can be picked up at the Cathedral ticket office.

■ Ta' Rikardu *(see p105)* is a popular choice for a snack.

TOP 10 ⭐ Dwejra, Gozo

The western tip of Gozo is beautiful, with wild, wave-battered cliffs, dramatic rock formations and wind-whipped headlands. This stretch of coastline, known as Dwejra, is blessed with celebrated natural landmarks such as Fungus Rock. It was also home to the famous Azure Window, which was sadly lost during a storm in 2017. The area is considered one of the finest in the Mediterranean for diving and snorkelling, and the cliffs are etched with walking paths offering panoramic views. In summer the sea is a calm and perfect blue, but in winter huge waves dash dramatically against the cliffs.

1 Dwejra Point
This dramatic promontory at Gozo's most westerly point used to be dominated by a towering rock arch, the Azure Window, once the most photographed sight on Gozo. Unfortunately the arch collapsed during a storm in 2017.

2 Inland Sea
Formed long ago by the collapse of a vast cave, this shallow lagoon **(below)** is always calm and a perfect place for a swim. It is also the starting point for the Dwejra boat trips.

5 Dwejra Bay
The sweeping bay **(above)** curving around Fungus Rock is a good place for swimming as the shallow rocks offer easy access. It's also a popular yacht anchorage.

3 Boat Trips
Fishermen run trips from the Inland Sea to Dwejra Point through a curious rift in the cliff. The journey is short but exhilarating. Even without the Azure Window the trip is still worth it.

4 Wildlife
Despite instances of illegal hunting, the Dwejra cliffs remain an important bird breeding and nesting site. The Fungus Rock is also home to the rare Maltese wall lizard.

NEED TO KNOW

MAP C1

■ Try to visit at dusk if possible; a sunset at Dwejra is unforgettable.

■ Take a picnic and enjoy it by the seashore or savour restaurant dishes on your way to the Inland Sea.

8 Diving and Snorkelling

Dwejra is a marine protected area that is popular with divers and snorkellers **(left)**. The Malta Tourism Authority website *(see p113)* has details of dive centres in the area. A small exhibition *(see p58)* allows you to see marine life without getting wet, using videos, models and panels.

THE GENERAL'S ROCK

Fungus Rock, also known as "The General's Rock" in Maltese, was named after the Italian general who accidentally fell to his death on its slippery cliffs. The plant was referred to as "General's Root" or the Maltese Fungus and was thought to cure dysentery, staunch bleeding and prevent infections. Hence, the rock was kept under constant watch to deter thieves. While modern science has revealed that the plant has no medicinal value, the rock remains protected for reasons of conservation.

---

10 Blue Hole

The Blue Hole **(above)** is another remarkable natural phenomenon close to Dwejra Point: a chimney, about 10 m (33 ft) wide and 25 m (82 ft) long, which links the open sea with the Inland Sea through an underwater arch. It's an extremely popular dive site.

6 Chapel of St Anne

This simple little chapel overlooks the Inland Sea. Built in 1963 on the site of a much older church, it is rather dishevelled but important to local people.

7 Dwejra Tower

This squat little watchtower was erected by the Knights in the 16th century to guard Fungus Rock, or "The General's Rock". A hoist was constructed to winch an official plant-gatherer across to the rock, which was very difficult to scale.

9 Fungus Rock

The strange rock **(below)** in Dwejra Bay gets its name from a rare plant, *Cynomorium coccineum*, that still grows there. The Knights prized the plant highly: anyone caught stealing it was sentenced to three years in the galleys. The rock remains out of bounds to this day.

TOP 10 ★ Comino

Comino is a diminutive but paradisiacal island with a permanent population of just three, and no main streets or shops. It takes just a couple of hours to make a circuit of the island, taking in dramatic cliffs and rocky coves where other visitors – even in the height of summer – rarely penetrate. Comino's most famous attraction is the dazzling Blue Lagoon; it's best to stay overnight in the island's one hotel if you want to enjoy its turquoise waters in peace.

① Blue Lagoon

This glorious natural inlet divides Comino from the islet of Cominotto. Its clear waters are quiet and sheltered, making them popular with families.

② The Village

This ramshackle building **(above)**, behind Comino Tower, was an isolation hospital in the early 20th century. It now houses Comino's few remaining inhabitants.

③ Santa Marija Bay

Comino's second sandy beach is overlooked by a few pink bungalows, a pink police station and a whitewashed chapel. It's perfect for swimming and snorkelling.

NEED TO KNOW

MAP A1

Our Lady's Return from Egypt: 2155 6826; open Sat evening and Sunday morning; call to check

■ Boats run between Ċirkewwa and Mġarr (all year round; it takes 25 mins (€5). Guests at Comino Hotel *(see p115)* are given preference, but the ferry can be used by non-residents (Round trip: €10; children €5).

■ Comino Hotel has a restaurant and snack vans, but the best option is to bring a picnic.

④ Our Lady's Return from Egypt

This charming chapel overlooking Santa Marija Bay was built in the 13th century. Its simple bell tower and whitewashed walls are reminiscent of Greek island chapels.

⑤ Wildlife

Comino is one of the few places in the area where the hunting ban *(see p110)* is generally respected, and there are bird-watching opportunities, particularly in the spring. For a dry island there is diverse plant life.

7 Comino Tower

The most imposing building on Comino is a crenellated watchtower **(left)** guarding the sea passage between Malta and Gozo. It was erected by order of Grand Master Alof de Wignacourt in 1618 and was restored in 2002, retaining many of the original features.

THE SPANISH MESSIAH

The great dream of the Spanish Jew Abraham ben Samuel Abulafia (1240–c.1292) was to create a new religion that would unify Jews, Christians and Muslims. Most people thought he was, at best, insane or, at worst, a heretic. He travelled to Rome, hoping to convert Pope Nicholas III, who died of apoplexy before carrying out his threat to burn Abraham at the stake. After this escape and a spell in Sicily, Abraham withdrew to a cave on the uninhabited island of Comino for three years. He wrote two texts setting out his ideas, but little is known of his later years.

9 St Niklaw Bay

This pretty bay with clear waters is one of only two sandy beaches on Comino, but non-guests of the Comino Hotel must pay a fee to use it.

10 St Mary's Battery

This sturdy battery was built by the Knights in 1714 as part of a chain of coastal defences across the Maltese islands. It was topped with a semicircular gun platform, but the cannons mounted there were never fired. It is now used as a lookout to protect migratory birds.

6 Crystal Lagoon

Just beyond the Blue Lagoon, this natural inlet **(above)** is fringed by steep cliffs. As a result the Crystal Lagoon can only be accessed by boat. The incredibly clear waters also make it a popular snorkelling site.

8 Cominotto

A tiny islet facing Comino, Cominotto **(below)** is located across the Blue Lagoon. It has a tiny stretch of beach (at low tide you can wade across from Comino), and its rocky coastline is riddled with numerous caves. It's one of the best diving spots in the area.

The Top 10 of Everything

Re-creation of Sweethaven, Popeye's
hometown, at Popeye Village, Anchor Bay

🔟 Moments in History

① 5000 BC–2500 BC: Prehistoric Malta

Human settlement in Malta dates back to 5200 BC when farmers arrived from Sicily to set up homes in caves like Għar Dalam (see p43). The first of the islands' great temples were built around 3600 BC. The temple period came to a mysterious end in 2500 BC.

② 800 BC–AD 4th century: Tarxien Cemetery, Bronze Age, Phoenicians, Carthaginians and Romans

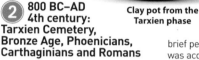

Clay pot from the Tarxien phase

A Copper Age culture, known as the Tarxien Cemetery phase, lived here after the temple culture ended, and this in turn was followed by the Bronze Age of defensive settlements. The Phoenicians arrived in around 800 BC, and the Carthaginians used the islands as a military base from the 6th century BC until their defeat by the Romans in 218 BC. Legend alleges that St Paul was shipwrecked on Malta in AD 60, initiating the country's history of religious devotion.

③ AD 4th century–1090: Byzantine and Muslim Eras

After the division of the Roman Empire in 395, Malta came under the control of the Byzantines until their defeat by the Arab caliphs. The Arabs left their mark both on agriculture and on the language. The islands fell to Roger I, the Norman Count, in 1091.

④ 1090–1282: Medieval Malta

The Maltese had relative independence under Norman rule, and many continued to practise Islam. In 1194, control of the islands passed to the Swabian kings, who expelled the Muslims forever. After a brief period of French rule, Malta was acquired by Spain in 1282.

⑤ 1282–1530: Spanish Rule

Under the Aragonese and later the Castilians, the first local governing body, the Università, was created and the first Maltese nobles were appointed. Charles V gave the islands to the Knights of St John in 1530.

⑥ 1530–1798: Knights of Malta

The Knights built Valletta, along with many palaces, fortifications, and engineering works such as the Wignacourt Aqueduct. They defeated the Turks in the Great Siege of 1565, which was a fatal blow to Muslim aims in the central Mediterranean.

The Great Siege of 1565

7 1798–1800: French Rule

In 1798, Napoleon took Malta from the Knights without a struggle. He stayed just six days, but his troops remained and stripped the islands of valuables. The outraged Maltese revolted and sought British help. The French were then defeated and the British took control.

8 1814–1939: British Rule

After defeating the French, the British declared Malta a colony in 1814 at the Treaty of Paris. It grew wealthy as an important refuelling station for British steamships on their way to India. In World War I, Malta was used as a vast hospital.

Valletta after a bombing raid, WWII

9 1939–1945: World War II

Due to its strategic location, during World War II Malta became the most bombed place on earth – 6,700 tons fell in just six weeks. The brave Maltese were awarded the George Cross in 1942 "to bear witness to a heroism and devotion that will long be famous in history".

10 1945–21st Century: Post-War Malta

Much of Malta lay in ruins after the war, although the British gave funds for reconstruction. The yearning for independence grew stronger and was finally granted in 1964. In 1979, the last British forces left the islands. Malta joined the EU in 2004.

TOP 10 WORLD WAR II SITES

Replica WWII bomb, Mosta Dome

1 Unexploded Bomb, Mosta Dome
In the dome is a replica of the bomb that pierced the roof during Mass, but miraculously failed to explode (see p90).

2 Siege Bell Memorial, Valletta
MAP K2
Standing at the tip of Valletta, this huge bell commemorates victims of 1942's Second Great Siege.

3 War Memorial, Floriana
MAP H3
This bears the names of 2,297 British Commonwealth servicemen.

4 George Cross Medal, National War Museum, Valletta
The George Cross (see p40) was awarded to the Maltese people in 1942 for their heroism during World War II.

5 Lascaris War Rooms, Valletta
The defence of Malta and the invasion of Sicily were planned here (see p67).

6 "Faith" biplane, National War Museum, Valletta
Of three old World War II biplanes, "Faith", "Hope" and "Charity", only "Faith" has survived (see p40).

7 Malta at War Museum, Birgu
This interesting museum offers a tour of one of the largest underground shelters in Malta (see p25).

8 Red Tower, Marfa Ridge
This 17th-century fortress was used as a British signalling station (see p82).

9 Ta' Qali Airfield
Now disused, the main wartime airfield is home to a crafts village and the Malta Aviation Museum (see p92).

10 Dockyard Creek, Birgu
MAP K4
HMS Illustrious, a symbol of bravery to the Maltese, was moored here.

🔟 Museums

Gallery at the National Museum of Archaeology

① National Museum of Archaeology, Valletta

A visit to this archaeology museum is essential to fully understand Malta's unique early history. Star attractions include the Horus and Anubis pendant, bronze daggers and a ceramic anthropomorphic sarcophagus from the Phoenician period *(see p65)*.

② Fortifications Interpretation Centre, Valletta

MAP H2 ▪ Triq San Mark ▪ 2122 8594 ▪ Open Summer: 9am–1pm Mon, Wed & Fri (to 4pm Tue & Thu); Winter: 10am–4pm Mon, Wed & Fri (to 7pm Tue & Thu); 9:30am–1pm Sat

Games, 3D puzzles and a multilingual guide are part of the exhibition held in this magnificent building – a brilliant day out for all the family.

③ Museum of St John's Co-Cathedral, Valletta

On display here are treasures of the Knights, including vestments, portraits of Grand Masters (look out for Antoine de Favray's rendition of the decadent Pinto), tapestries and the monstrance built to hold the reliquary of the right hand of St John the Baptist. Part of the museum has undergone reno-vation and is due to reopen at full capacity in 2018 *(see pp14–17)*.

④ Cathedral Museum, Mdina

Alongside the expected Maltese and Italian reli-gious paintings here are a rare set of prints by the German artist Albrecht Dürer (1471–1528). Other notable exhibits include fine church silver, a bishop's carriage and a remarkable collection of Malta's coins, from the Carthaginians to the 20th century *(see p21)*.

⑤ National War Museum, Fort St Elmo, Valletta

MAP K1 ▪ Fort St Elmo ▪ 2123 3088 ▪ Open 9am–5:30pm daily ▪ Adm

Fort St Elmo was the first target of the Turks in the Great Siege. It has been fully restored to house the refur-bished National War Museum. The museum has interesting multimedia displays and original objects ranging from Eisenhower's jeep and the George Cross to the table on which the French surrender was signed.

⑥ Lascaris War Rooms, Valletta

This fascinating museum is located in military operation rooms deep in the bastions of Valletta. It was used by the British as a secret headquarters during World War II and by NATO during the Cold War in the 1960s to monitor Soviet submarines *(see p67)*.

The underground Lascaris War Rooms

⑦ Malta Maritime Museum, Birgu

Exhibits here range from model ships to lavish ceremonial barges built for the Grand Masters (see p25). Look out for the traditional decorations from fishing boats, including a wonderful St George and the dragon.

⑧ MUŻA – National Museum of Arts, Valletta

Highlights include works by Mattia Preti (1613–99) and a watercolour of Valletta by the British artist J M W Turner (1775–1851), who never set foot in the islands. The museum is currently closed until late 2018, when it will reopen at a new location in the Auberge d'Italie (see p65).

Interior of MUŻA

⑨ Ġgantija Interpretation Centre, Gozo

MAP E1 ▪ 2155 3194 ▪ Open 9am–4:30pm daily

The Centre at Ġgantija displays the key finds from the 5,000-year-old temples (see p101) and the nearby Neolithic burial ground, the Xagħra Hypoguem (see p102), plus significant finds from other prehistoric sites. The Centre connects visitors to the site of the temple via a pathway, with views of the surrounding landscape.

⑩ Malta at War Museum, Birgu

The Malta at War museum includes original items in enlightening displays and a tour through one of Malta's largest underground shelters, plus a remarkable British documentary film with footage of Malta at war (see p25).

TOP 10 ARTISTS AND ARCHITECTS

Gafa's St Pauls Cathedral, Mdina

1 Francesco Buonamici (1490–1562)
This celebrated Italian engineer was responsible for designing Valletta's first major Baroque buildings.

2 Gerolamo Cassar (1520–92)
Cassar was the architect commissioned to design the Grand Masters' Palace and St John's Co-Cathedral.

3 Francesco Laparelli da Cortona (1521–71)
The Pope sent Laparelli da Cortona (who was once Michelangelo's assistant) to oversee the building of Valletta.

4 Matteo Perez d'Aleccio (1547–1616)
This former pupil of Michelangelo created the Great Siege frieze in the Grand Masters' Palace.

5 Tommaso Dingli (1591–66)
Dingli designed many of Malta's most beautiful Renaissance churches, including St Mary's in Attard.

6 Mattia Preti (1613–99)
Painter of the nave in St John's Co-Cathedral, Preti was considered by many to be Malta's finest artist.

7 Lorenzo Gafa (1638–1703)
An outstanding Baroque architect, Lorenzo Gafa designed both the Mdina and Gozo cathedrals.

8 Andrea Belli (1703–22)
Belli remodelled the Auberge de Castille for Grand Master Pinto, adding superb Baroque flourishes.

9 Antoine de Favray (1706–91)
This French-born artist's portraits and landscapes can be viewed at the National Museum of Arts.

10 Edward Lear (1812–88)
Best-known for nonsense poems, Lear was an accomplished watercolourist who loved the landscape of Malta.

🔟 Temples and Ancient Sites

1 "Clapham Junction"

Curious pairs of grooves or cart ruts, etched into the limestone, can be found across Malta. The earliest ruts are likely to be Bronze Age. They have never been fully explained, but probably relate to some form of transport. The sheer number of ruts here, at Misrah Ghar il-Kbir, have earned it the nickname "Clapham Junction", after the busy London train station (see p90).

Cart ruts at "Clapham Junction"

2 Ġgantija, Xagħra, Gozo

One of the best-preserved Neolithic sites on the islands, Ġgantija is in a wonderful setting overlooking Gozo's central plateau. The oldest temple was built in 3600 BC, while the younger was tucked in next to it a few years later (see p101).

3 Ta' Ħaġrat, Mġarr

Two temples form this small complex. The larger, built in 3600–3000 BC, is one of the earliest on the islands, while the smaller dates to 3300–3000 BC. The view of Mġarr rising behind the temple ruins is charming (see p81).

4 Ħaġar Qim, Qrendi

Ħaġar Qim sits on a limestone acropolis. A remarkable cache of "Fat Lady" (goddess-like) figures was found here, as well as a fine decorated stone altar (see pp18–19).

5 Tarxien, Paola

One of the latest temple complexes on the islands, Tarxien is probably the most decorated (see p95). Finds include a huge "Fat Lady" and complex reliefs. An altar containing a flint knife and animal bones suggests sacrifice. Heritage Malta are working to improve accessibility and protect the remains.

6 Mnajdra, Qrendi

Of all the temples, Mnajdra most captivates visitors. Thanks partly to its breathtaking coastal setting little changed since it was built. A set of three typically designed temples, Mnajdra's alignments have caused the site to be described as a "calendar in stone" (see pp18–19).

Prehistoric Ġgantija temples on Gozo

⑦ Ħal Saflieni Hypogeum, Paola

One of Europe's most extraordinary prehistoric sites, Ħal Salflieni is a vast underground burial complex carved from solid rock *(see pp28–9)*.

Visitors touring the Għar Dalam Cave

⑧ Għar Dalam Cave and Museum, Birżebbuġa

The "Cave of Darkness" was home to some of Malta's first human inhabitants from over 7,000 years ago. This exceptional site is also the source of an amazing collection of fossils showing that dwarf elephants, hippos and giant dormice once roamed these islands *(see p95)*.

⑨ Skorba, Żebbiegħ

This small temple complex is, along with Ġgantija in Gozo, one of the oldest free-standing buildings in the world (though there is not much left to see here). Initially excavated in the 1960s, the site was undisturbed by earlier, less careful explorations. It was built on an even older village site; very early depictions of the human figure, now displayed in Valletta's Museum of Archaeology *(see p65)*, were found here *(see p81)*.

⑩ Xagħra Circle, Gozo

MAP E1 ■ Not open to the public ■ www.heritagemalta.org

This important underground burial site *(see p102)*, undisturbed by earlier excavators, has provided some extraordinary data, human remains and artifacts, the most important of which are on display at the Ġgantija Interpretation Centre *(see p41)*.

TOP 10 ARCHAEOLOGICAL FINDS

1 "Sleeping Lady"
This statue of a sleeping woman was made around 3000 BC and found in the Ħal Saflieni Hypogeum *(see pp28–9)*.

2 Venus of Malta
Unlike the stylized "Fat Ladies" from many temples, the Maltese Venus of Ħaġar Qim is extraordinarily realistic.

3 Red Skorba Figurines
The earliest representations of the human figure in Malta were a group of small female figurines found at Skorba.

4 Two Fat Ladies
Discovered at the Xagħra Circle on Gozo, these two ladies are sitting on a carefully carved couch.

5 Shaman's Bundle
This intriguing group of stick figurines *(see p31)*, human and animal, was discovered at the Xagħra Circle on Gozo.

6 Snake Relief
A huge stone unearthed at Ġgantija is etched with an undulating snake. Its significance is still a mystery.

7 Bird Potsherd
This delicate Ġgantija potsherd has a repeating pattern of a crested bird.

8 Animal Friezes
Sheep and pigs, all handsomely carved in relief, strut across a pair of stone blocks discovered at Tarxien.

9 Tarxien Altar
This stone altar, with spiral decoration, has a secret compartment where a flint knife and animal bones were found.

10 Giant Goddess of Tarxien
Only the lower half of this giant statue, perhaps the most striking "Fat Lady," survives. A replica is on site at Tarxien.

Giant Goddess replica, Tarxien

🔟 **Churches and Cathedrals**

Frescoed interior of St Paul's Cathedral

① St Paul's Cathedral, Mdina

Mdina's cathedral is said to stand on the site of the villa of Roman Governor Publius, converted to Christianity by St Paul. Lorenzo Gafa designed today's elegantly restrained Baroque structure after an earthquake destroyed the original (see p20–21).

② St Paul's Shipwreck Church, Valletta

For many, the arrival of St Paul on the islands in AD 60 is the single greatest event in Maltese history. In the depths of this ornate Baroque church (see p66), which is dedicated to Malta's famous patron saint, is a fragment of the pillar on which St Paul is said to have been beheaded and a much-venerated relic of the saint's wristbone.

③ Church of St Lawrence, Birgu

Knights and the Maltese celebrated the end of the Great Siege here in 1565. Lorenzo Gafa designed the present church in 1681, and it was restored after being badly damaged in World War II (see p24–5).

④ Xewkija Rotunda, Gozo

Completed in 1971, Xewkija Rotunda is said to have the third-largest dome in Europe – but this is disputed by the people of Mosta (see p45). The church can hold three times Xewkija's population (see p102).

⑤ Our Lady's Return from Egypt, Comino

Set back from Santa Marija Bay, this winsome little church dates from the 13th century. The simple whitewashed building is topped with three hooped bells and surrounded by a grove of tamarisk trees. Mass is said twice a week (see p34).

⑥ St John's Co-Cathedral, Valletta

One of Valletta's most iconic sights, designed by Gerolamo Cassar, St John's Co-Cathedral was built as the Knights' conventual church. It is lavishly decorated inside and conceals many treasures (see pp14–17).

Ta' Pinu Basilica set in open countryside

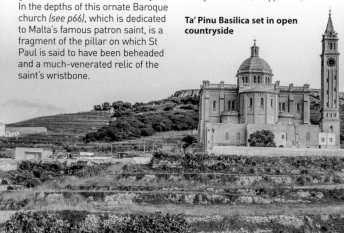

7 Parish Church of Senglea (L-Isla)

The original 18th-century church was destroyed in World War II but has been restored *(see p74)*. Dedicated to Our Lady of Victories, it has a wooden statue of the Virgin Mary encased in silver, plus a memorial to those who lost their lives in World War II.

8 Mosta Dome, Mosta

The huge dome of Mosta's parish church (officially Our Lady of the Assumption) was built from 1833 to 1871. It is argued that the dome is the third largest in Europe *(see p90)*.

Side view of Gozo Cathedral

9 Gozo Cathedral, Victoria

Lorenzo Gafa designed this elegant Baroque cathedral, with its wonderful *trompe l'oeil* dome, standing at the heart of the Citadel *(see p31)*.

10 Ta' Pinu Basilica, Gozo

Thousands of Maltese travel here annually hoping that Our Lady of Ta' Pinu will cure their ailments *(see p103)*. Ex-voto offerings, from crutches to plaster casts, show the strength of their belief.

TOP 10 RELIGIOUS FIGURES

Sculpture of St John the Baptist

1 St John the Baptist
St John has been patron saint of the Knights since the Order was founded.

2 St Agatha
A patron saint of Malta, St Agatha is said to have hidden from her Roman persecutors in a cave in Rabat Victoria.

3 St Publius
Roman governor Publius, converted to Christianity by St Paul, was appointed first Bishop of Malta.

4 St Paul
In AD 60, St Paul was shipwrecked off the islands; he then went on to convert the local populace to Christianity.

5 Pope Pius V
Pius V helped pay for the construction of Valletta and sent his best engineers to advise on the project.

6 Our Lady of the Assumption
The most popular incarnation of the Virgin Mary in Malta. Her feast day, on 15 August, is one of the liveliest *festas*.

7 Our Lady of Ta' Pinu
Our Lady of Ta' Pinu is credited with miraculous healing powers and many make the journey to the Basilica *(see p103)* in search of a cure.

8 Saint Peter
The feast of saints Peter and Paul on 29 June has fused with the traditional Maltese festival of Mnarja *(see p61)*.

9 San Lawrenz
San Lawrenz is unique as the only patron saint to have a Maltese village named after him, in Gozo.

10 St Andrew
Patron saint of fishermen. St Andrew's statue appears in lamp-lit niches across the islands. There's also a statue on the seafront in Xlendi.

TOP 10 Grand Masters

Portrait of L'Isle Adam

1 Philippe Villier de L'Isle Adam (1521–34)

L'Isle Adam was Grand Master when, in 1522, the Turks defeated the Order of St John and ousted it from Rhodes. The Knights then spent the next eight years looking for a permanent home until Charles V of Spain offered them the Maltese islands.

2 Jean Parisot de la Valette (1557–68)

A brave and charismatic man, La Valette led the Knights in the Great Siege of 1565; he was 70 years old. He responded to Turkish attacks by firing back the heads of Turkish prisoners. After the victory, he began to build the city that now bears his name.

3 Jean l'Evêque de la Cassière (1572–81)

La Cassière commissioned the building of St John's in Valletta as the conventual church of the Order. Only in 1816 was it granted Co-Cathedral status.

4 Alof de Wignacourt (1601–22)

Wignacourt's term of office was notable for the construction of several coastal fortifications, including the St Lucian Tower at Marsaxlokk and the Wignacourt Tower in St Paul's Bay. He also provided much of the funding for a new aqueduct to bring water from Rabat to Valletta (see p92).

5 Jean de Lascaris Castellar (1636–57)

The Maltese still use the phrase wiċċ Laskri (face of Lascaris) for a sour facial expression, after this famously dour man. Like Wignacourt, he commissioned watchtowers and fortifications around the island, such as the Red Tower on Marfa Ridge (see p82).

6 Nicolas Cotoner (1663–80)

Nicolas Cotoner followed his brother Raphael (Grand Master 1660–63). Together, these two Spanish Knights were responsible for the lavish decoration of the interior of St John's Co-Cathedral. Nicolas also strengthened the city walls, and ordered the construction of the Cottonera Lines and Fort Ricasoli, both of which protect the Three Cities (see pp72–5).

7 Antoine Manoel de Vilhena (1722–36)

The Knights generally had as little as possible to do with the locals, but this Portuguese Grand Master was an exception. De Vilhena did all he could to improve the lives of the Maltese people, and as a result achieved great popularity. He was responsible for building the suburb of Floriana (just

Bronze statue of Antoine Manoel de Vilhena

outside Valletta), the exquisite Manoel Theatre, Vilhena Palace in Mdina and Fort Manoel in Marsamxett Harbour.

⑧ Manoel Pinto de Fonseca (1741–73)

This vain, flamboyant and shrewd Grand Master gathered a huge court, which vied with the most fashionable in Europe. Under his rule, many of Valletta's restrained Renaissance buildings were embellished, including the Grand Master's Palace and the Auberge de Castille. He died at the age of 92, and rumour has it that he owed his longevity to the elixirs concocted by his private alchemist.

Inside the Grand Master's Palace

⑨ Ferdinand von Hompesch (1797–79)

Von Hompesch was an amiable Grand Master, but unsuited to a stand-off with a cunning leader like Napoleon. He oversaw the cession of Malta to the French, without a single shot being fired. When Napoleon was defeated at Waterloo, Malta became British.

⑩ Fra' Giacomo dalla Torre del Tempio di Sanguinetto (2017–)

After the 79th Grand Master resigned in a dispute with the Vatican, Giacomo dalla Torre del Tempio di Sanguinetto will serve as Lieutenant ad interim.

TOP 10 UNUSUAL FACTS ABOUT THE KNIGHTS

Silver pitcher and plate

1 Dining off Silver
Invalids in the Knights' Hospital dined off silver plates, for ease of cleaning.

2 Flamboyant Pinto
Among Pinto's staff was a baker whose only responsibility was to make bread for the Grand Master's hounds.

3 English Knight
Sir Oliver Starkey, English secretary to La Valette, is the only Knight below Grand Master buried in the crypt of St John's.

4 The Maltese Falcon
The Knights paid an annual tribute of a live falcon to the King of Spain – the historical nugget that inspired Dashiell Hammett's celebrated story.

5 Dragut Rais and La Valette
These heroes, on opposing sides during the Great Siege of 1565, had both previously spent time as galley slaves.

6 The Oubliette
Wrongdoers were confined in this dark hole in the rocks beneath Fort St Angelo.

7 Sex and Croquet
To keep his Knights free of impurity, Grand Master Lascaris made them play *palla a maglio*, a version of croquet.

8 Valletta, Party Capital
By the 18th century, piety forgotten, Valletta gained a reputation for its promiscuity and hedonism.

9 Important Relics
When the Knights left Malta in 1798 defeated by Napoleon *(see p17)*, they took the hand of St John the Baptist and other important relics with them.

10 Sovereign Knights of the Order of Malta
The Order of the Knights no longer have a permanent territory, but claim sovereign (state-like) status.

🔟 Areas of Natural Beauty

Reddish sands at San Blas Bay

of salt. The pools, glassy in winter and oddly pale in summer, have a peculiar yet haunting beauty *(see p104)*.

③ Dwejra, Gozo
Spectacular cliffs, rocks with supposedly magical powers and curving bays make this famous stretch of Gozitan coastline among the most scenic regions in the Maltese islands *(see pp32–3)*.

④ Ta' Ċenċ Cliffs, Gozo
These sheer, silvery cliffs are hauntingly lovely, particularly at dusk. Wonderful walking trails follow the line of the cliff edge, and the pock-marked limestone landscape is etched with the mysterious Bronze Age "cart ruts". Although illegal hunting remains a problem in the area, these cliffs are home to pro-tected sea and coastal birds, including the blue rock thrush *(see p102)*.

① San Blas Bay, Gozo
This secluded little beach can be found at the end of a lush valley filled with fruit trees, and its reddish sand makes a striking contrast with the green of the orchards. There is no direct road for access and just one kiosk in summer, so it is normally wonderfully peaceful *(see p104)*.

② Salt Pans, Gozo
The salt pans, which are located between Xwieni Bay and Reqqa Point, are formed by shallow indentations in the creamy limestone, right on the water's edge. In winter storms, the pans fill with sea water, which evaporates in the summer heat to leave behind chunky white crystals

⑤ Marfa Ridge
At the very northern end of Malta, Marfa Ridge is the wildest and least populated part of the island. It was historically impossible to defend, which explains why few settlements grew up here. The rocky coast is dotted with pretty little bays and beaches – the best are Paradise Bay and Little Armier *(see p84)* – and the towering cliffs of Ras Il-Qammieh rear up at the southwestern end. Understandably, the area is very popular with hikers *(see p82)*.

Salt pans next to the sea

6 Fomm Ir-Riħ Bay

This wild and remote bay is surrounded by gentle hills featuring tumbling terraces of pale stone. The only way to get down to the bay is via a steep stone staircase hacked into the rock. As a result, it has one of the few beaches in Malta that remains relatively uncrowded in the summer (see p84).

7 Dingli Cliffs

A thrilling road skirts these cliffs, 300 m (1,000 ft) high, which plunge into the inky sea. This is the loveliest and least spoiled corner of Malta, and is beautiful during spring and autumn when the fields are carpeted with wild flowers. Take a picnic of fresh Maltese bread, tomatoes and some pungent local cheese with you (see p89).

Blue Grotto hidden beneath the cliffs

8 Blue Grotto, Wied Iż-Żurrieq

This huge natural arch in the cliffs, located near the tiny village of Wied Iż-Żurrieq, gets its name from the unearthly blue that seems to flicker beneath the waters, evoking thoughts of the mermaids who were believed to live here. There is a boat trip available that takes in a number of other sea caves along the same stretch of coast (see p96).

9 Buskett Gardens

In a fairly barren island, the Buskett Gardens stand out as Malta's most extensive woodlands. Perfect for picnics and leafy walks, these woods are the scene of one of Malta's most enjoyable festivals, Mnarja (see p61). They were first established as a hunting ground for the Knights, and are filled with groves of olives, citrus trees and plump, bushy pines that look like gigantic broccoli (see p90).

10 Blue Lagoon, Comino

The beautiful Blue Lagoon is formed by a narrow channel that cuts between the small island of Comino and minute Cominetto. The stunning azure waters are shallow and inviting, perfect for swimming, snorkelling and diving. Go out of season if possible, because the lagoon's languid charms can be shattered in summer by the crowds and the motor boats (see p35).

Yacht anchored on the Blue Lagoon

🔟 Walks and Drives

The rugged Comino coastline with St Mary's Tower in the distance

1 Circuit of Comino (walk)
MAP A1

This 8-km (5-mile) walk starts at the Blue Lagoon. Take the dirt road to Santa Marija Bay and follow the headland to the highest point of Comino. Walk towards St Mary's Battery, then continue around the coast to the Comino Tower (St Mary's) and back to the Blue Lagoon.

2 Delimara Point (walk)
MAP F6

A circular 8-km (5-mile) walk beginning at Marsaxlokk. Make for the bay of Il-Ħofra Żgħira, follow the coast to Peter's Pool for a dip, then to Delimara Point. Return the other side for views of Marsaxlokk Bay.

3 Xlendi to San Lawrenz, Gozo (walk)
MAP D2

Although arduous, this 12-km (7-mile) walk includes the stunning Dwejra Cliffs. From Xlendi Bay, climb up Tar-Riefnu and continue to Wardija Point. Follow the track to Dwejra Bay, then the path by the chapel to San Lawrenz.

4 Marfa Ridge (walk)
MAP B2

A 14-km (9-mile) circuit from Mellieħa Bay takes in Marfa Ridge. Head for the Ras il-Qammieħ cliffs, follow the coast to Ċirkewwa and Aħrax Point, and then head back around the coast.

5 Wied Il-Għasri and Salt Pans, Gozo (walk)
MAP D1

This is a circular 12-km (7-mile) route from Victoria (Rabat). Head for Għasri, then follow the signs for the Wied Il-Għasri, a blaze of colour in spring. Follow the coastline towards Marsalforn to see the salt pans scooped from limestone, and from Marsalforn walk back to Victoria.

6 Victoria Lines: Fomm Ir-Riħ to Baħar iċ-Ċagħaq (walk)
MAP A4

This 30-km (19-mile) coast-to-coast hike follows the ruins of the Victoria Lines, British-built fortified walls. Begin at Fomm Ir-Riħ (or at Mġarr if relying on public transport), and follow the walls to Baħar iċ-Ċagħaq.

A segment of the Victoria Lines wall

⑦ Floriana (walk)
MAP G3

Floriana is a town of faded Baroque beauty located right at the gates of Valletta. Begin this short 1.5-km (1-mile) tour by strolling along the Mall, then continue to the Sarria Chapel, decorated by Mattia Preti. Wander through the Botanic Gardens before visiting the Lion Fountain and turning back towards Valletta.

⑧ Siġġiewi to Dingli (walk)
MAP C5

This 10-km (6-mile) walk takes in the stunning Dingli Cliffs. Begin in Siġġiewi, pass the chapel of Tal-Providenza, and reach the cliffs at the Underground Chapel. Follow the cliffs to the giant golf ball of Dingli radar station. Continue on to Dingli to pick up the bus back to Siġġiewi.

Ramla Bay viewed from Calypso's Cave

⑨ North Coast, Gozo (drive)
MAP D2

From Victoria (Rabat), head for pretty Għarb and the Ta' Pinu Basilica, then on to Żebbuġ. Lunch in Marsalforn, then drive east to Calypso's Cave and Ramla Bay to swim, then return via Xagħra to Victoria.

⑩ West Coast, Malta (drive)
MAP D6

From Qrendi, follow the road to the Ħagar Qim and Mnajdra temples. Drive on narrow roads to Laferla Cross, then follow signs for the "Clapham Junction" cart ruts and to enjoy a breathtaking cliff view. Continue via the cliff road to Dingli.

TOP 10 VIEWPOINTS

Upper Barrakka Gardens

1 Upper Barrakka Gardens, Valletta
These beautiful gardens, with their pretty fountains and flowers, frame magnificent views over the stunning Grand Harbour (see p58).

2 Dingli Cliffs Viewpoint
At the halfway point on the cliff road along Dingli Cliffs is a viewpoint. Park and walk to the headland (see p89).

3 Red Tower, Marfa Ridge
This crenellated tower on the ridge offers views over much of Malta and across to Comino and Gozo (see p82).

4 Citadel Walls (Victoria), Gozo
Climb to the very top of the Citadel's ramparts for amazing views over Gozo's verdant central plain (see p30).

5 Xewkija Rotunda, Gozo
The lift in Xewkija's church takes you to the top of the huge dome for stunning views over all of Gozo (see p102).

6 Qammieh Point, Marfa Ridge
The massive cliffs of the wild coastline stretch in both directions (see p82).

7 Dwejra Point, Gozo
Gozo's western coast, with its mighty cliffs and natural rock formations, looks beautiful from this high point (see p32).

8 Mdina's Ramparts
From Mdina's ramparts (see p20) you can see some major landmarks, including the enormous Mosta Dome.

9 Senglea Tower
This curious tower, in tiny gardens on the tip of L-Isla, offers lovely views of Valletta across the Grand Harbour.

10 Wignacourt Tower, St Paul's Bay
MAP C3
This lookout tower, built by the Knights, affords far-reaching views.

🔟 Outdoor Activities

1 Diving and Snorkelling
PDSA: MAP E4; Msida Court, 61
Msida Sea Front; info@pdsa.org.mt
Maltese waters are renowned for diving and snorkelling. Natural harbours, bays, wrecks, reefs and caves offer endless opportunities for experienced and novice divers alike. The water is warm and clear, and there is a wealth of marine life. Use one of the licensed dive centres listed on the Malta Tourism Authority website (see p113).

2 Hiking
Both Malta and Gozo boast excellent hiking trails (see pp50–51); Gozo has the edge because it is less crowded. Comino is also great for a hike, if only because few visitors venture beyond the bays. Watch out for Maltese hunters (see p110).

Climbers tackling the sheer cliffs

Hiker on the cliffs above Għar Lapsi

3 Sailing
Malta has a maritime tradition dating back thousands of years, and yachting is still very popular. The biggest marinas are to be found in Marsamxett Harbour (see p108).

4 Other Watersports
Most hotels can arrange jet-skis, water-skiing, parasailing, windsurfing and so on. The best windsurfing areas are Mellieħa and Baħar iċ-Cagħaq. Water polo is a popular spectator sport – in fact, it's a national obsession.

5 Rock Climbing
Malta Climbing Club: 9929 9836; www.maltaclimbingclub.com
There are no mountains, but the cliffs offer exciting challenges for climbers. More than 1,200 established routes include climbs suitable for people of all abilities. The Malta Climbing Club offers advice on the best spots.

6 Boat Excursions
Many boat excursions are available, from a tour of Valletta's Grand Harbour and trips to Comino's Blue Lagoon to jaunts taking in all three main islands. In Malta, most trips start from Sliema or Mellieħa Bay. In Gozo, most tours begin at Mġarr Harbour.

7 Horseriding

Malta has a long tradition of horseriding, and boasts Europe's oldest polo club. There are several stables where you can arrange children's pony rides or treks for experienced riders. Malta's Tourism Authority website *(see p113)* can supply a list of approved centres.

8 Kayaking

Gozo Adventures: MAP D2; Triq Santa Marija, Victoria Gozo; 9999 4592; www.gozoadventures.com
Venture out on crystal blue waters, perfect for kayaking, and explore the scenic shorelines of Malta and Gozo.

9 Bird-Watching

Illegal Hunters and trappers have done their best to wipe out the Maltese bird population, but they haven't succeeded. They eliminated the Mediterranean peregrine falcon from the beautiful Ta' Ċenċ cliffs, but this area is still home to all kinds of birdlife, including the largest colony of breeding Cory's shearwaters in the Maltese islands. There are two bird sanctuaries in Malta *(see p83)*.

10 Golf

Royal Malta Golf Club: MAP D4; Triq Aldo Moro, Marsa; 2122 3704; www.royalmaltagolfclub.com
Malta has just one golf course, the Royal Malta Golf Club. It is open to visitors daily except Thursday and Saturday mornings, but advance booking is essential. Facilities include a bar, restaurant, pro shop, practice-putting green and driving range. Equipment can be hired, and lessons are available for golfers of all abilities.

A boat excursion to Comino island

TOP 10 DIVING AND SNORKELLING SITES

Diving at Santa Marija Caves

1 Santa Marija Caves, Comino
MAP A1
There are several caves, some offering spectacular swim-throughs.

2 Ahrax Point
MAP B2
Off Marfa Ridge, the huge seaweed meadows shelter abundant marine life. There is good visibility for photos.

3 Blenheim Bomber, Marsaxlokk
MAP F5
The remains of this World War II plane make for an interesting but difficult dive.

4 Delimara Point
This site is reached by boat. Groupers and stingrays are often seen *(see p27)*.

5 Fungus Rock, Gozo
Several good sites cluster around Dwejra; this huge rock, covered in marine life, is one of the best *(see p33)*.

6 Dwejra Point, Gozo
Another scenic dive at Dwejra. Boulders shelter abundant marine life *(see p32)*.

7 The Blue Dome, Gozo
MAP D1
Light reflects onto the vast ceiling, creating the "blue dome" effect. Fish include sea horses.

8 San Dimitri Point, Gozo
MAP C1
Accessible only by boat. There are shoals of barracuda and other fish.

9 Lighthouse Reef, Comino
MAP A1
Perhaps Comino's best site, with a chimney through the reef. Marine life includes sea horses and starfish.

10 Marfa Point, Ċirkewwa
MAP B2
This site is good for night dives, and also has a training pool for beginners.

🔟 Children's Attractions

1 Malta Experience, Valletta

MAP K2 ▪ St Elmo Bastions, Triq Il-Mediterran ▪ 2552 4000 ▪ Shows: on the hour 11am–4pm Mon–Fri, 11am–2pm Sat, Sun (to 1pm Sun Jul–Sep) ▪ Adm ▪ www.themalta experience.com

Malta has countless audiovisual attractions, mostly located in Valletta and Mdina, but this is one of the best. The Malta Experience offers an informative and entertaining introduction to the 7,000-year history of the islands on a giant screen. But the 45-minute show may be a bit too long for smaller children.

Old plane at Malta Aviation Museum

2 Malta Aviation Museum

Kids will enjoy seeing the large collection of vintage aircraft on display at this fun museum. The more technically minded can watch volunteers restoring the planes (see p92).

Families having fun at Popeye Village

3 Gozo Citadel

This car-free maze of narrow limestone streets is a perfect place for older children to roam and discover. Circumnavigate the citadel on top of the bastion walls and visit graffiti-clad prison cells, a gunpowder store and a World War II shelter, before relaxing on the grass in the historic defensive ditch (see pp30–31).

4 Buġibba Water Park

MAP C3 ▪ St Paul's Bay, Islet Promenade ▪ Open 10am–7pm daily

This fun park on the resort waterfront has 17 water features to spray, splash and soak kids in the summer sun. The large square enclosure is divided into three separate areas for different-aged children, and there are free 20-minute sessions.

5 Eden SuperBowl

Ten-pin bowling can provide a welcome respite from soaring temperatures or rainy days (see p77).

6 Popeye Village, Anchor Bay

This colourful attraction for the young at heart was created here for the movie, Popeye. Also known as Sweethaven (Popeye's hometown), fun activities include a boat trip around the harbour, silversmiths, mini-golf, a fun-pool, a small playground and the chance to be a cast member in the movie (see p82).

Fish tanks, Malta National Aquarium

⑦ Malta National Aquarium

MAP C3 ■ Triq it-Trunciera, San Pawl il-Bahar ■ 2258 8100 ■ Open 10am–7:30pm daily ■ Adm ■ www. aquarium.com.mt

A captivating walk-through tank and 130 different species of fish make this a wonderful place to visit with children. The outdoor play area is a welcome added attraction.

⑧ Mellieħa Beach

This popular, sandy and shallow bay is particularly suitable for families with small children (see p84).

⑨ Playmobil Fun Park, Ħal Far

MAP E6 ■ Ħal Far Industrial Estate ■ 2224 2445 ■ Open 10am–6pm (to 10pm Fri & Sat) ■ www.playmobil malta.com

Kids aged six-plus can tour the world's second-largest Playmobil factory and see all their favourite characters being made. Book the factory tour ahead.

⑩ Captain Morgan Underwater Safari

MAP Q3 ■ Buġibba, next to Bognor Beach ■ Departs at 11am, 1pm & 3pm; Mon–Sat Jun–Sep, Mon–Fri Apr, May & Oct ■ Adm ■ www.captain morgan.com.mt

Take a trip on a glass-bottomed boat and see how many types of fish you can spot. The trip takes just over an hour and includes fish-feeding.

TOP 10 CHILD-FRIENDLY RESTAURANTS

1 The Avenue, Paceville
Kids will love this colourful, buzzy budget restaurant (see p79).

2 Henry J Beans American Bar & Grill, St Julian's
MAP D3 ■ Corinthia San Ġorġ, St George's Bay ■ 2370 2694
This 1950s-style burger-and-rib joint features an outdoor terrace.

3 Piccolo Padre, St Julian's
MAP P2 ■ 194/5 Triq It-Torri ■ 2134 4875
A popular Italian restaurant serving great pasta and pizzas.

4 Hard Rock Café, St Julian's
MAP N1 ■ Bay Street Hotel Tourist Complex, St George's Bay ■ 2138 0983
The rock-themed decor here features Cher's dress, and the menu offers the usual burgers and fajitas.

5 Tal-Familja, Marsaskala
This friendly seafood spot is a firm favourite with local families (see p99).

6 Mamma Mia
MAP E4 ■ Ta' Xbiex Seafront ■ 2133 7248
Friendly ambience, efficient service and delicious Mediterranean food.

7 Blue Creek, Għar Lapsi
Overlooking the lido, this restaurant is very family-friendly (see p99).

8 Tex Mex Grill & Cantina, Sliema
MAP P3 ■ 89 Triq ix-Xatt ■ 2133 9247
This rather raucous US-themed spot is always a big hit with youngsters.

9 Gillieru, St Paul's Bay
A great family-friendly choice overlooking the bay (see p85).

10 Fontanella Tea Gardens, Mdina
Kids like these outdoor tea rooms for their delicious cakes (see p93).

Terrace at Fontanella Tea Gardens

🔟 Culinary Highlights

Fenek stew, a popular dish on restaurant menus

1 Fenek
The most popular meat in Malta, *fenek* (rabbit) is a favourite for *festas* and special events. It is prepared in countless ways, but the most common include rabbit stew made with wine and flavoured with herbs, rabbit fried with garlic and herbs, and a simple dish of spaghetti served with a rabbit sauce.

2 Torta Tal-lampuki
This fish pie is made with *lampuki*, a prized local fish that is only available for a relatively short period each year (usually mid-August to December). Such is the demand for this fish that rights to catch it are granted by lottery. The pie combines the fish with vegetables, walnuts, olives and raisins, and is considered a great delicacy by locals.

Traditional *hobz biz-zejt*

3 Pastizzi and Qassatat
Malta's favourite snack, *pastizzi* are tasty, mini pasties stuffed with ricotta cheese or a pea mixture. *Pastizzi* stalls can be found everywhere, and virtually every old-fashioned bar will offer its own, homemade versions. *Qassatat* are similar to *pastizzi* but made of a lighter pastry and round in shape.

4 Gbejniet
These small round cheeselets are typical of Gozo and are made from goat or sheep's milk. There are two common kinds: the plain, which is smooth and creamy, and the peppered version, which is piquant and perfect with the local crusty bread and a slice of tomato. These cheeses are often used to flavour other dishes, such as soups.

5 Soppa Tal-armla
Maltese cuisine boasts many delicious soups, including *minestra* (vegetable soup) and the traditional *soppa tal-armla* (literally "widow's soup"). This name probably comes from the simple ingredients, which include potatoes, courgettes and other vegetables, plus a dollop of ricotta cheese or a *gbejniet* cheeselet.

6 Hobz biz-zejt
These are thick slices of bread brushed with olive oil and topped with a sweet tomato paste, onions, olives and capers. They were traditionally a humble snack, akin to Italian *crostini*, but have acquired a sophisticated cachet and some variants include cheese, tuna or anchovies.

7 Maltese Bread

The Maltese are justly proud of their excellent bread. Most villages have at least one bakery, where you can pick up delicious *hobz* (small soft rolls) or *ftira* (a ring-shaped loaf that is similar in texture to Italian *ciabatta*).

8 Bragioli

Similar to the Italian version of "beef olives", *Bragioli* are made using slices of beef or veal stuffed with a mixture of cheese, ham and herbs, then braised gently on the stove or in the oven.

Bragioli, stuffed beef rolls

9 Mqaret

These scrumptious pastry parcels (usually diamond-shaped), are filled with a date mixture and deep-fried. They make the perfect sweet snack, and are delicious, if fattening.

10 Qubbajt

This nougat-style sweet is made with almonds and honey, and is traditionally eaten at festivals and special events. There are always several stalls selling *qubbajt* at village *festas*, but it is also available year-round from stalls and local shops. It is said to date back to the Arab occupation of the islands.

A shop in Mdina selling *qubbajt*

TOP 10 RESTAURANTS

Traditional ambience at Rubino

1 Rubino, Valletta
Once a confectionery shop, Rubino is still famous for its desserts *(see p71)*.

2 Giannini, Valletta
This place offers beautiful harbour views while you dine on creative Maltese and Italian cuisine *(see p71)*.

3 Da' Pippo, Valletta
This small friendly trattoria serves typical local and Mediterranean food *(see p71)*.

4 Ta' Frenc, Xaghra, Gozo
Housed in a 14th-century farmhouse, the award-winning cuisine here uses ingredients from the farm *(see p105)*.

5 Ta' Karolina, Xlendi
Set on the water's edge, this place serves great fish, meat and pizzas *(see p105)*.

6 Ta' Rikardu, Victoria
An ideal place for a simple meal washed down with local wine *(see p105)*.

7 Angelica, Valletta
A bright restaurant that serves delicious rabbit stew cooked in champagne *(see p71)*.

8 Guzé, Valletta
Locals head to Guzé for the romantic ambiance and the unmissable warm chocolate pudding *(see p71)*.

9 La Reggia, Marsaxlokk
Lunch at this delightful waterfront restaurant is a must for anyone visiting Marsaxlokk *(see p99)*.

10 Barracuda, St Julian's
Outstanding Mediterranean cuisine is served in the spectacular setting of a historic villa overlooking the water *(see p79)*.

⑩ Malta for Free

① PANACEA Environmental Education Centre, Dwejra, Gozo

MAP C1 ▪ Near Inland Sea ▪ 2156 3556 ▪ www.panaceaproject.net

Dwejra is a marine protected area on the western tip of Gozo that is popular with divers and snorkellers. This exhibition takes you under the water without getting wet. Marine life and landscape can be seen in underwater videos, interactive panels, resin replicas and a diorama.

② San Anton Palace and Gardens, Attard

Built in the early 17th century by Grand Master Antoine de Paule, the palace is now the summer residence of the president (not open to visitors). The British opened the gardens to the public in the 1880s and they remain a public park with shady paths, ponds, terrapins, a maze and an aviary *(see p90)*.

③ Fortifications Interpretation Centre, Valletta

Find out all you need to know about Fortress Malta, with particular focus on the fortifications of the Knights of St John, at this museum housed in a converted 16th-century Knights' warehouse. Highlights include a children's exhibition, interactive screens and a 3D model. Learn all about it inside, then step outside and walk the bastion walls themselves *(see p40)*.

④ Church of Our Lady of Victories Chapel, Valletta

MAP H3 ▪ Triq Nofsinhar

This was the first church in Valletta and it was named in honour of the Madonna, who was believed to have aided the Knights' victory in the Great Siege of 1565. A Baroque façade was added later, along with 18th-century interior decoration. Jean de Valette was buried here until St John's was completed.

Bone relic, St Paul's Shipwreck Church

⑤ St Paul's Shipwreck Church, Valletta

The Bible tells how St Paul was shipwrecked on Malta in 60 AD, converting the nation to Christianity. This venerated church contains a relic of St Paul's wrist bone and part of the stone column on which he is said to have been beheaded in Rome, as well as a stunning Mattia Preti altarpiece *(see p66)*.

⑥ Upper Barrakka Gardens

MAP H3 ▪ Triq Sant' Orsla ▪ Open 7am–10pm daily

Perched on top of Valletta's bastion walls, this arcaded terrace and small pleasure garden full of monuments affords stunning panoramas of the Grand Harbour, as well as vertiginous views of the capital's fortifications. Built by the Knights and cherished by the British, it is a pleasant place to take a rewarding breather from a day of sightseeing.

7 **Mass in St John's Co-Cathedral**

On Sunday morning, the great west doors of this extraordinary Baroque edifice open to all for sung Mass. This is not the time for photos and audio-guides but the ideal opportunity to see the cathedral beautifully candlelit and used as it was intended – without having to pay the usual admission charge (see pp14–17).

8 **Walking Trails**

Malta's tourist offices (see p112) have a set of free booklets showing walking routes across the country. Complete with maps, public transport details and information on the sights passed, they take you off the beaten track to discover hidden bits of history and stunning views. The coast of Gozo is particularly attractive.

9 **Verdala Palace and Buskett Gardens**

More a small forest than a garden, Buskett was created for the hunting pleasure of the Knights. The palace (not open to the public) looks like a castle but was more for leisure than defence (see p90). The Maltese love to picnic here in summer, particularly for the Mnarja festival (see p61).

10 **"Clapham Junction" and Dingli Cliffs**

The Dingli Cliffs (see p89) are a wonderful place to walk amid some stunning scenery (particularly the view from the 17th-century chapel). Inland, explore troglodyte caves and "Clapham Junction" – grooves in the limestone thought to have been formed by long-lost vehicles shifting stones from ancient quarries (see p90).

View out over the sea from Dingli Cliffs

TOP 10 MONEY-SAVING TIPS

Open-air market in Marsaxlokk

1 Visit markets and roadside vendors to stock up on fresh produce and local delicacies for picnic meals.

2 If you can, visit in April or October rather than summer peak season. The prices are much lower at these times of year, sights are less crowded and it is still hot enough to sunbathe.

3 The bus services on Malta and Gozo are good and extremely cheap so you shouldn't need taxis or rental cars.

4 Book the Hypogeum (see p28) online in advance. The earlier you book, the less you will pay, and if you leave it too late you might miss out altogether.

5 Get the Malta Pass. You pay for the card upfront (and can choose from a one-day, two-day or three-day option) but it will give you access to 40 top attractions, making it great value if you plan to cram a lot in.

6 Buy bottled water from local shops – it will be far cheaper than if you pay for water through your hotel.

7 It is often more affordable to stay in self-catering apartments rather than opting for a package, all-inclusive hotel deal.

8 Take a free walking tour. There are several companies in Valletta that offer this, such as Colour My Travel (tips are usually expected at the end of the tour).

9 Dine in one of the food kiosks lining the beaches. These offer generous portions of a surprisingly good selection of dishes at bargain prices.

10 Look out for open days at museums and heritage sites when major archaeological sites and museums waive admission. Details of all open days are available at www.heritagemalta.org.

🔟 Festivals and Events

Locals dressed in flamboyant costumes at the Carnival parade

① Valletta Baroque Music Festival

Two weeks in Jan ▪ www.valletta baroquefestival.com.mt

For two weeks each year, Valletta's Baroque theatre, churches and palaces ring with the sounds of music of the same period. Top international and local musicians perform, often on period instruments.

② Carnival
Feb

The Knights brought Carnival to Malta in the 16th century. It takes place in the week leading up to Ash Wednesday, and has always been an excuse to let off steam before Lent begins. It is celebrated in villages across the islands with parades,

fireworks and fancy dress. The biggest events are in Valletta and Floriana; Nadur, in Gozo, is infamous for its own rather unruly version.

③ Good Friday
Mar/Apr

Malta is staunchly Catholic, and Good Friday is marked with suitable solemnity. Statues of scenes from the Passion of Christ are paraded through the streets all over the islands.

④ Easter Sunday
Mar/Apr

In contrast to sombre Good Friday, Easter Sunday is a joyful affair. There are more parades, but they include music and sometimes even fireworks. *Figolli* (pastry figures filled with marzipan) are exchanged, along with chocolate eggs and rabbits.

⑤ Fireworks Festival, Valletta
Late Apr

The Maltese love fireworks, and every year they show off their prowess using the Grand Harbour as the theatre. Other countries are invited to participate, and for three consecutive nights the Grand Harbour is ablaze with colour and sound. It is not to be missed if you are in the islands.

A Good Friday procession in Mosta

6 Local Festas
Throughout summer

Every village in Malta and Gozo celebrates the feast day of its patron saint with gaudy lighting and street decorations, brass bands, parades, firework shows, traditional foods and plenty of local wine. Each village competes to put on the best *festa*.

7 Isle of MTV
Jun ■ www.isleofmtv.com

A highlight of the Malta Music Week, this event has been graced by the likes of Jessie J and Lady Gaga. Youngsters and music lovers throng Floriana, outside Valletta, to watch live performances by top artists.

8 Mnarja
28/29 Jun

This traditional folklore festival is celebrated with music, dance, song and local foods such as *fenkata* (rabbit stew). The main arena is Buskett Gardens, where there are bareback horse and donkey races, and traditional singing known as *Ghana*.

9 Jazz Festival, Valletta
Jul ■ www.maltajazzfestival.org

Major international performers are invited to the three-day jazz festival held on Barriera Wharf, in the Grand Harbour. The setting is magical, and a variety of musical styles entertain.

A Maltese Christmas crib scene

10 Christmas Celebrations
Dec

A country with a population that is mainly Catholic, Malta celebrates Christmas with gusto. Beautiful lights adorn the city of Valletta and in some years a village is turned into a live re-enactment of the nativity scene.

TOP 10 FESTIVAL TRADITIONS

Fireworks light up the sky at *festa*

1 Fireworks
At the heart of every village *festa* are fireworks; Lija and Mqabba are famous for their wonderful displays.

2 Traditional Foods
Local nougat *(qubbajt)* is eaten at all festivals. During Mnarja, it's traditional to eat rabbit *(fenek)*, and at Easter, marzipan-stuffed pastry *figolli*.

3 Pilgrimages
The devout Maltese make pilgrimages to holy sites such as St Paul's Grotto in Rabat or the Ta' Pinu Basilica in Gozo.

4 Penitents
Following the floats of Easter processions, penitents are barefoot, dressed in white robes with pointed hoods and carry big, heavy crosses.

5 Folk Dances
Folk dances are performed in traditional dress. Among them are *il-Maltija* and the *parata*, performed with sticks.

6 Floats
The Maltese take decorations for festivals very seriously. Carnival floats are particularly flamboyant.

7 Confetti
On village feast days, children toss confetti from balconies as the main statue from the church is paraded.

8 Street Decorations
Maltese street decorations are literally dazzling. Lines of light bulbs outline the church and often the houses too.

9 Brass Bands
The British introduced this tradition, which is enthusiastically embraced.

10 Petards
For weeks leading up to the local summer *festas*, children tear around the villages letting off these fire crackers.

Malta and Gozo
Area by Area

Ta' Pinu Basilica, standing on the outskirts of the village of Għarb

🔟 Valletta

The European Capital of Culture 2018, this glorious city of golden stone straddles a promontory flanked on either side by natural harbours. Built for the Knights after the Great Siege of 1565, Valletta is contained behind a ring of impenetrable walls, it's skyline pierced by spires and domes such as that of Carmelite Church. The city's heart is broad Triq Ir-Repubblika, which is lined with princely palaces and dominated by the Co-Cathedral of St John. From here, side streets flanked by palazzi slope down to the harbours. Neglect and World War II bombing have all taken their toll on the capital, but its cobbled streets remain hauntingly redolent of the era of the Knights.

Statue, National Museum of Archaeology

VALLETTA

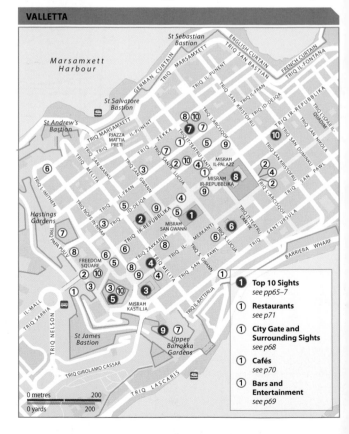

| | **Top 10 Sights** see pp65–7 |
| **Restaurants** see p71 |
| **City Gate and Surrounding Sights** see p68 |
| **Cafés** see p70 |
| **Bars and Entertainment** see p69 |

1 St John's Co-Cathedral

Severe and unembellished on the outside, inside St John's Co-Cathedral explodes in a glorious visual paean to the wealth and influence of the Knights *(see pp14–17)*.

2 National Museum of Archaeology

MAP H2 ▪ Triq Ir-Repubblika ▪ 2122 1623 ▪ Open 9am– 4:30pm daily ▪ Adm ▪ www. heritagemalta.org

The old Auberge de Provence, its former magnificence somewhat battered, houses this collection of fascinating artifacts gathered from Malta's prehistoric temples *(see p40)*. One of the star attractions is the serene "Sleeping Lady" *(see p28)*.

3 Auberges of the Langues
MAP H3

Each of the eight *Langues*, national branches of the Order of St John, had its own inn, or auberge, in 16th-century Valletta. They were grand lodging houses for the Knights, and monuments to their wealth and prestige. Most of the few surviving auberges are not open to the public, but their graceful Baroque façades epitomize Valletta's regal allure. The most lavish is the Auberge de Castille et Leon (on Misrah Kastilja), now the office of the Maltese president.

Baptism of Jesus by Mettia Preti, MUŻA

4 MUŻA – National Museum of Arts

MAP H3 ▪ Auberge D'Italie ▪ 2122 5769 ▪ Closed for renovation ▪ Adm

Inside the historic Auberge of the Italian Knights, MUŻA is the flagship project of Valletta's year as European Capital of Culture 2018 and will re-open by the end of the year *(see p41)*.

5 St James Cavalier Centre for Creativity

MAP H3 ▪ Pjazza Kastilja ▪ 2122 3200 ▪ Open 10am–1pm Sat & Sun ▪ www. kreattivita.org

One of the bastions that protect the main gate into the city has been beautifully restored. It now houses this centre for contemporary arts, with a theatre, cinema and galleries. There's also a café, Inspirations *(see p70)*, with an outdoor terrace.

The elaborate façade of the Auberge de Castille, one of the eight *Langues*

Exquisite ceiling that adorns the inside of St Paul's Shipwreck Church

6 St Paul's Shipwreck Church

MAP J2 ■ Triq San Pawl ■ 2122 3348 ■ Open 6:30am–12:30pm, 3–6:30pm Mon–Sat; 7am–noon, 4–6pm Sun

This elaborate church was built between 1639 and 1740 by Gerolamo Cassar *(see p41)* on the site of an earlier church *(see p44)*. The façade was added in 1885 by Nicola Zammit.

The auditorium of the Manoel Theatre

7 Manoel Theatre

MAP J2 ■ Triq It-Teatru L'Antik ■ 2122 2618 ■ Guided visits every 45 minutes, 10am–4pm Mon–Fri, 10am–noon Sat ■ Adm ■ www. teatrumanoel.com.mt

Around the corner from the dominant dome of Carmelite Church, the Manoel is one of the oldest working national theatres in the world, and was built in 1731 by the order of Grand Master António Manoel de Vilhena. The auditorium comprises five levels, orchestra stalls, a gallery and three tiers of boxes painted with a gilded Mediterranean scene. A lavish box at the centre of Tier I was reserved for the Grand Master, but is now used by the Maltese president. The adjoining museum contains 19th- century machinery for making dramatic sound effects. The café is one of the nicest in Valletta *(see p70)*.

8 Grand Master's Palace

This spectacular palace is filled with opulent tapestries and paintings, and was the magnificent residence of the Grand Masters of the Order of the Knights of St John for more than two centuries *(see pp12–13)*.

MALTA AND THE MOVIES

Valletta's Grand Harbour is spectacularly cinematic, ringed by honey-coloured spires and bastions that have barely changed in centuries. The Maltese islands have provided the backdrop for countless films, including *Troy*, *Gladiator*, *Midnight Express*, *The League of Extraordinary Gentlemen*, *Swept Away*, *A Different Loyalty* and *Popeye*.

⑨ Lascaris War Rooms
MAP H3 ■ St James Ditch
■ 2123 4717 ■ Open 10am–4:15pm
daily ■ Adm

Wartime atmosphere is re-created with models and equipment in these dank, sunless rooms that were once the nerve centre for military operations during World War II *(see p40)*. General Eisenhower and Field Marshal Montgomery were among the Allied commanders based here.

⑩ Casa Rocca Piccola
MAP J2 ■ 74 Triq Ir-Repubblika
■ 2122 1499 ■ Guided visit only, on the hour 10am–4pm Mon–Sat ■ Adm
■ www.casaroccapiccola.com

This exquisite palace was built in the 16th century for an Italian Knight, but it has belonged to the noble de Piro family for the last two centuries. The 9th Marquis de Piro has opened his family home to the public, and entertaining guided tours are available around the 50-room palazzo. The rooms contain some beautiful items of furniture and quirky curios, such as a pouch of medical instruments – among the very few silver objects to survive Napoleon's rapacious troops. There's also an ornate 18th-century sedan chair. The family portraits and photographs lend the house a warm and personal ambience.

Blue Room, Casa Rocca Piccola

▶ MORNING

Take a bus to the **Triton Fountain** facing the city entrance and head through the main gate. Sweep down **Triq Ir-Repubblika** *(see p68)* to **St John's Co-Cathedral** *(see pp14–17)*, the most splendid church in the Maltese islands. After visiting the cathedral, have a coffee out on the square at the **Caffe Cordina** *(see p70)*. Continue down Triq Ir-Repubblika to the **Grand Master's Palace** *(see pp12–13)*, once the residence of the Grand Master. Have a snack at one of the cafés on Triq Il-Merkanti before stopping by the **Manoel Theatre**. Lunchtime concerts are often held here – check in advance with the tourist office for times.

AFTERNOON

Return to Triq Ir-Repubblika and make for the Auberge de Provence, home to the fascinating **National Museum of Archaeology** *(see p65)*. A visit will help you to put Malta's extraordinary temple culture into context. Don't miss the Bronze and Phoenician galleries or the mysterious sculpture of the "Sleeping Lady." Stroll over to the **Upper Barrakka Gardens** *(see p58)*, which are small but beautifully kept, for spellbinding views over the Grand Harbour. The view is best at dusk, extending across the water to the romantic silhouette of the Three Cities *(see pp72–5)*. Take the elevator down to **Valletta waterfront** and walk along the shore to pick your preferred bar or restaurant. End your day with a visit to the charming **Casa Rocca Piccola** for an evening champagne tour with Nicholas, the Marquis (book in advance).

See map on p64 ⬅

City Gate and Surrounding Sights

1 City Gate Defences
MAP H3

Valletta was built to be impregnable and this is clear at City Gate, the main entrance into the capital. Vast bastion walls tower over a deep ditch. The bridge was originally a drawbridge.

2 The New Gateway
MAP H3

The brand new 21st-century gateway, designed by Renzo Piano (the architect of London's Shard), was designed to welcome people in rather than close them out. It is part of Piano's renovation of the whole City Gate area.

3 City Gate Steps
MAP H3

Piano created flights of steps inside the bastion walls giving new access to the top of the fortifications, the cavalier and Hastings Gardens. Buskers gather at the steps.

4 Triq Ir-Repubblika (Republic Street)
MAP H3–J2

This is Valletta's main street running from City Gate to Fort St Elmo at the end of the Valletta peninsula. Halfway down is the main square and the Grand Master's Palace (see pp12–13).

5 Pjazza Teatru Rjal
MAP H3 ■ Triq In-Nofsinhar ■ 2247 8100 ■ www.pjazzateatrurjal.com

Opened in 2013, this open-air theatre by Renzo Piano is set inside the remains of Malta's Neo-Classical National Opera House, which was bombed in World War II.

6 Freedom Square
MAP H3

Freedom Square inside City Gate is a great place for a first taste of Malta's characteristic *gallariji* – enclosed painted wooden balconies that overhang many of its narrow traditional streets and squares.

7 St James and St John Cavalier
MAP H3 ■ Pjazza Kastilja

These two vast gun emplacements guard the landward side of Valletta. St James is now a contemporary arts centre (see p65). Enter up the atmospherically lit stone staircase flanked by hugely thick walls.

8 Statue of Jean de Valette
MAP H3

The Grand Master of the Knights of St John – the man after whom the city is named – is commemorated in this statue, which was erected in 2012 on the piazza of the same name.

9 Church of St Catherine of Italy
MAP H3 ■ Victory

Originally the Church of the Italian Knights, this 16th-century church has a 17th-century Baroque façade and a beautiful octagonal interior. The altarpiece is by Mattia Preti.

10 Parliament
MAP H3

Malta's first purpose-built parliament, designed by Renzo Piano, was opened in 2015. Faced with local stone, it reflects the earlier architecture of Valletta and is lifted on stilts.

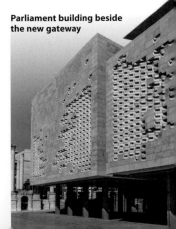

Parliament building beside the new gateway

Bars and Entertainment

Alfresco setting at the Bridge Bar

1 Bridge Bar
MAP J3 ■ Triq Sant' Orsla

Frequented by patrons from the art world, this alfresco bar is particularly favoured on summer evenings. It also stages live music performances.

2 The Pub
MAP J2 ■ Triq l-Arċisqof

This tiny hole-in-the-wall pub has a ghoulish claim to fame: it is here that Oliver Reed is said to have drunk himself to death during the filming of the movie *Gladiator*. A collection of photos of the actor adorn the walls.

3 Trabuxu
MAP G4 ■ 1 Triq Id-Dejqa

Black-and-white photos of musical instruments cover the brick walls of this subterranean wine bar. Laid-back and stylish, it's a great spot to unwind after a hard day's sightseeing.

4 StrEat
MAP J2 ■ Triq Id-Dejqa

This bar is visited by the post-theatre crowd for whiskey and late-night snacks. It hosts parties that go on until the early morning hours.

5 Tico Tico
MAP J2 ■ Triq Id-Dejqa

Vintage photographs embellish the walls of Tico Tico, an intimate lounge bar. It has played a major role in helping a former red-light area earn a name for its thriving nightlife.

6 Charles Grech
MAP J2 ■ Triq Ir-Repubblika

Frequented by MPs, this is one of Valletta's favourite café-bars. It has a smart ambience but is relaxed and is not over-priced. It serves snacks, good coffee and a wide selection of spirits.

7 Legligin
MAP H2 ■ 119 Triq Santa Lucija

An atmospheric wine bar offering a good range of local and international wines that can be enjoyed with a selection of Maltese food.

8 Manoel Theatre

This tiny jewel of a theatre *(see p66)* is the ideal place for an atmospheric night out. Its stage has presented several major international performers. The courtyard café *(see p70)* is perfect for a light lunch.

9 Kingsway Bar & Café
MAP J2 ■ 57 Triq Ir-Repubblika

This bar, with a chic and relaxed atmosphere, serves great food platters and spectacular cocktails.

Entrance to St James Cavalier Centre

10 St James Cavalier Centre for Creativity

Valletta's arts centre offers a range of activities for the whole family, from cult-film screenings to theatre and dance performances *(see p65)*.

See map on p64 ←

Cafés

The interior of Caffe Cordina, a local institution

(5) Kantina Café
MAP J2 ■ Pjazza San Ġwann

Around the corner from St John's Co-Cathedral, this café serves tempting food and delicious cakes. It also has a substantial drinks menu.

(6) Piadina Caffe
MAP J3 ■ 24 Triq Santa Lucija

The place for healthy lunchtime snacks, Piadina's charming owner has made this a popular spot. Great hot chocolate is served here.

(1) Caffe Cordina
MAP J2 ■ 244 Triq Ir-Repubblika

Valletta's most famous café, the elegant Cordina has a large, shady terrace on the square. The drinks and snacks (which include *pastizzi*) are pricey, but the location is worth it.

(2) Café Jubilee
MAP H2 ■ 125 Triq Santa Lucija

Small and wood-panelled, with tiny booths, this cosy spot is decorated with vintage posters. It is a favourite with locals who come here for the tasty sandwiches and light meals.

(3) Inspirations
MAP H3 ■ Triq Il-Kavallier ta' San Ġwann

Part of the St James Cavalier Centre for Creativity (see p65), Inspirations offers tasty Maltese and Italian dishes plus lighter fare such as soups and quiches. There's a pretty terrace.

(4) St James Cavalier Centre for Creativity Café
MAP H3 ■ Pjazza Kastilja

This casual café, with old-time prints and curios on the walls, is a popular place for breakfast or a mid-morning snack. Be sure to try a cappuccino and a couple of ricotta-filled *pastizzi*.

(7) Upper Barrakka Kiosk
MAP H3 ■ Triq Sant' Orsla

In the Upper Barrakka Gardens atop Valletta's bastion walls, this is the perfect place for a coffee break with the city sights laid out before you. Take a seat at one of the outdoor tables and enjoy the fabulous views.

(8) Reno's Café
MAP H3 ■ Triq San Zakkarija

Ideal for a leisurely cup of coffee, Reno's is also a great spot for a quick bite or a light snack. *Ftira* (Maltese bread) with a filling of scrumptious items from the deli counter is recommended as a takeaway.

(9) Culto Caffetteria
MAP H2 ■ Triq San Ġwann

Believed to serve one of the best coffees in Valletta, the tiny Culto Caffetteria also offers a wide selection of sandwiches and salads.

(10) Café Manoel
MAP J2 ■ 115 Triq It-Teatru L'Antik

This arty café is tucked in the Manoel Theatre's courtyard. It serves sandwiches, homemade soups and classic local dishes such as rabbit stew. Opera plays in the background.

Restaurants

PRICE CATEGORIES

For a three-course meal for one with half a bottle of wine (or equivalent meal), taxes and extra charges.

€ under €30 €€ €30–€50 €€€ over €50

1 LVB
MAP J2 ▪ 65/66 Triq Il-Merkanti ▪ 7928 5845 ▪ Closed Mon ▪ €€

Choose from three carefully crafted tasting menus, including a vegetarian option, which list Maltese dishes with French leanings.

2 Angelica
MAP J2 ▪ 134 Triq L-Arcisqof ▪ 2122 2777 ▪ €€

Located close to the Grand Master's Palace, this chic restaurant serves a range of delicious dishes such as Maltese rabbit cooked in champagne. It's small, so booking is a must.

3 Guzé
MAP J2 ▪ 22 Old Bakery Street ▪ 2123 9686 ▪ Closed Sun ▪ €€

Set in a romantic 16th-century building, the menu at Guzé focuses on seasonal local produce. The indulgent hot chocolate pudding is a must.

4 Ambrosia
MAP J2 ▪ 137 Triq L-Arcisqof ▪ 2122 5923 ▪ Closed Sun ▪ €€

This cool and elegant eatery tucked down a side street serves creative and beautifully fresh local cuisine in a welcoming and informal setting. Save room for the heavenly desserts such as lemon cheesecake.

5 Da' Pippo
MAP H2 ▪ 136 Triq Melita ▪ 2124 8029 ▪ Closed Sun L ▪ €

This tiny Italian trattoria offers a selection of traditional, delicious Maltese fare combined with excellent service. It is especially popular with business people at lunch, so booking ahead is recommended. Celebrities such as Tom Hanks have eaten here.

6 Giannini
MAP H2 ▪ 23 Windmill Street ▪ 2123 7121 ▪ Closed Sat L, Sun, Mon ▪ €€€

One of the finest restaurants in the capital, Giannini's offers sublime views to go with its sophisticated versions of local cuisine.

7 Rampila
MAP H3 ▪ St John Cavalier ▪ 2122 6625 ▪ €€

Steeped in Maltese tradition, this beautiful restaurant offers modern Mediterranean cuisine.

8 Rubino
MAP H2 ▪ 53 Triq Il-Fran ▪ 2122 4656 ▪ Closed Mon D, Sat L ▪ €€

This former confectionery shop is one of the best places for Maltese soups and stews.

The cosy dining room at Rubino

9 Crianza
MAP J2 ▪ 33 Triq L-Arcisqof ▪ 2123 8120 ▪ Closed Sun L ▪ €€

Housed in a vaulted cellar, this cheerful eatery is famous for its homemade ravioli, salads and grills.

10 Palazzo Preca
MAP H2 ▪ 54 Strait Street ▪ 2122 6777 ▪ Closed Sun L (winter), Mon ▪ €€

Run by two sisters, this fine-dining restaurant, in a 16th-century palazzo, is good for its pasta, fish and desserts.

See map on p64

TOP 10 Sliema, St Julian's and the Three Cities

Valletta's closest neighbours – Sliema and St Julian's to the northwest, and the Three Cities of Birgu (Vittoriosa), L-Isla (Senglea) and Kalkara to the southeast – couldn't be more different. The Three Cities, piled on two promontories jutting into the bay, are quiet, historic and time-worn, a far cry from the glitz of Sliema and St Julian's, where hotels, luxury apartments, shopping centres and nightclubs have mushroomed.

Church of St Lawrence in Birg

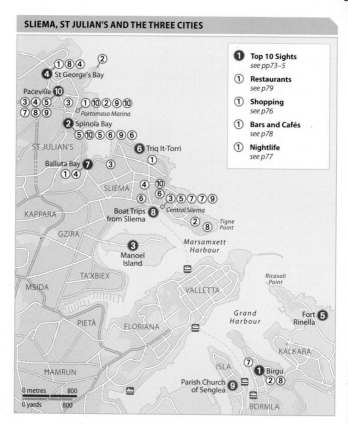

SLIEMA, ST JULIAN'S AND THE THREE CITIES

- **1** **Top 10 Sights**
  see pp73–5
- **1** **Restaurants**
  see p79
- **1** **Shopping**
  see p76
- **1** **Bars and Cafés**
  see p78
- **1** **Nightlife**
  see p77

1 Birgu

The Knights' first base in Malta, Birgu is a delightful little town standing on a peninsula that sticks out into the Grand Harbour. Fort St Angelo, the nation's oldest fortress, dominates the point of the peninsula while the Knights' and British buildings along the waterfront are now restaurants, cafés and the Malta Maritime Museum. Inland, enclosed within impressive fortifications, a maze of medieval streets includes the Collachio, the area once reserved for the Knights of St John and their auberges (see pp24–5).

2 Spinola Bay, St Julian's
MAP N1

There is little natural beauty in the concrete sprawl of Malta's northern coast, but Spinola Bay, with its smattering of pretty villas, is an exception. The small bay has become one of the most fashionable addresses in Malta. A clutch of smart restaurants overlook the bay. Multicoloured *luzzus* sway gently in the sun, as fishermen by the water's edge mend their nets. The bay is prettiest at night, when the water reflects the twinkling lights.

3 Manoel Island, Sliema
MAP G1 ■ Gzira

An island, but for a bridge linking it to Sliema, this largely abandoned area is full of history and due for restoration. The Knights used the island as a quarantine hospital from 1643. Shiploads of people were held here for weeks at a time to ensure they were not carrying the plague. Fort Manoel was built in the 18th century to guard Marsamxett Harbour.

4 St George's Bay
MAP N1

The only sandy beach in Sliema and St Julian's, St George's Bay is surrounded by bars, restaurants, clubs and fast-food joints, and is home to the Bay Street Mall (see p76). The sand is topped up with imports regularly, and the water is a typically clear-blue Mediterranean colour.

Historical re-enactment at Fort Rinella

5 Fort Rinella, Kalkara
MAP E4 ■ Triq Santu Rokku ■ 2180 0992 ■ Open 10am–5pm Mon–Sat ■ Adm ■ www.wirtartna.org

Rinella was one of a pair of coastal batteries built in the 1880s by the British, against threats from Italy. It was equipped with a huge Armstrong 100-ton gun, but the introduction of quick-firing guns 20 years later rendered this mighty weapon obsolete. A group of enthusiastic young men in Victorian garb stage an "animated tour" – letting off cannons and firing muskets – to provide an enjoyable insight into the fort's history.

Offshore view of Manoel Island

Independence Gardens on Triq It-Torri

6 Triq It-Torri, Sliema
MAP P2–Q2

Formerly a fishing village and modest resort, Sliema is now a dense concrete jungle packed with hotels, shops, restaurants and bars. But some old-fashioned traditions have survived – notably the *passeggiata*, the traditional evening stroll that was imported from Italy. Each evening, couples and families amble along the seafront, Triq It-Torri (Tower Road), nodding to neighbours and sizing up strangers. Pavement cafés make people-watching easier. The stretch from Ghar Id-Dud to St Julian's Point is the most popular.

7 Balluta Bay, St Julian's
MAP N2

Stand in front of the Meridien Hotel and, especially at night, Balluta Bay is an attractive waterside location

Waterside church at Balluta Bay

despite the rampaging tourist development of the 1980s and 1990s. Lots of restaurants – some excellent – and bars crowd the waterfront, some with lovely sea views. The clear waters in the bay are ideal for swimming, either from the rocks or a tiny foreshore, but there is no actual beach (go to St George's Bay for that). Water polo, a national obsession, is played in the lido on the edge of the water.

8 Boat Trips from Sliema
MAP Q3

Sliema – specifically the long quay known as Sliema Ferries – is the starting point for most of Malta's boat trips. Take a tour around the Grand Harbour and Marxamxett Harbour (the waters that surround Valletta). Or head off on a day trip to Comino and its Blue Lagoon, where you can also enjoy swimming and snorkelling in luminous blue waters, or explore the tiny island and surrounding caves. Another option is to get the ferry to Valletta from here, which is much quicker and nicer than going by road.

9 Parish Church of Senglea (L-Isla)
MAP K6 ▪ **27 Triq San Lawrenz**
▪ **2182 7203** ▪ **Open daily for Mass from 7am**

This parish church (also known as the Nativity of Mary) remains close to the hearts of the Maltese, thanks to the much-venerated statue encased in silver. In 1786, Pope Pius VI declared the church

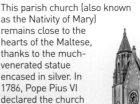

THE LOOKOUT

Out at the very tip of Senglea (L-Isla), the gardens of Ġnien Il-Gardjola contain a small but much-photographed *vedette* (lookout). Jutting out over the heights of Senglea Point, it frames a beautiful view of the Grand Harbour. The *vedette* is famously carved with symbols of vigilance: an eye, an ear and a crane. These were supposed to remind the sentries of their duty of watchfulness. The *vedette* was carefully dismantled and stored before World War II, and thus survived the bombs.

---

a "collegiate insignis" and it was given the title of Basilica by Pope Benedict XV in 1921. The church was destroyed by bombs in World War II but was rebuilt in 1956 *(see p45)*.

⑩ Paceville
MAP N1

Located just west of St Julian's, Paceville is Malta's nightlife capital. The mostly narrow streets are heavily populated with bars, pubs, clubs, hotels, and fast-food outlets. On a summer night the bass pounds and the streets are crowded with teenagers – the difference between dance floor and pavement can be somewhat academic (although it is now technically illegal to drink on the streets). The jollity continues well into the early hours. There are some excellent restaurants in the area too, which are frequented by all ages.

A WALK AROUND THE THREE CITIES

▶ **MORNING**

Enter **Birgu** *(see pp24–5)* through its mighty main gate (where there is a very nice outdoor café for a coffee break) and head along Triq Il-Mina l-Kbira. On the right, you'll come to the **Inquisitor's Palace**, where unfortunate prisoners were accused of heresy. Behind the Inquisitor's Palace is the original Knights' quarter, called the Collachio. Head down **Triq H Tabone** to see the auberges (inns) of the Knights, before returning to the central square, **Misrah Ir Rebh**. Turn right onto the **Vittoriosa Waterfront** and enjoy delicious food at any of the several good restaurants, many of which offer beautiful views of the yachts moored in the marina.

AFTERNOON

Wind your way down to the water's edge at Dockyard Creek. The **Freedom Monument**, in front of the Church of St Lawrence, commemorates those who died during World War II. Take a **boat tour** around the Grand Harbour (there are regular departures from the waterfront in Birgu) for sublime views of Valletta *(see pp64–71)* and the Three Cities. Continue your stroll around the bay, following the shoreline to the entrance to Senglea. Walk down Senglea's main street, **Triq Il-Vitorja** and branch right to visit **Parish Church of Senglea**. Continue down the main street to the **gardens** right at the tip of the promontory; here you will find the famous *vedette* (lookout) with its curious symbols, which offers more magnificent views.

See map on p72 ←

Shopping

1 Bay Street Mall, St Julian's
MAP N1 ■ St George's Bay

Visitors will be spoiled for choice in this stylish mall with branches of all the major chains (including most British and Italian high-street names), plus cafés and kids' play areas.

2 The Point, Sliema
MAP E4 ■ Tigne Point

Located in the modern Tigne Point, Malta's largest mall offers a wide variety of stores including many British upmarket names.

The Point shopping centre

3 Plaza Shopping Mall, Sliema
MAP Q3 ■ Triq Bisazza

Sliema's main shopping mall is spread over nine floors. It has high-street chains like The Body Shop and Benetton, along with cafés and a well-stocked bookshop, Agenda.

4 CamilleriParisMode, Sliema
MAP Q3 ■ Annunciation Square

Located close to the seafront, this elegant shop is known for the aesthetic quality of its products. A host of items ranging from home accessories to international delicacies are available here.

5 Merlin Library, Sliema
MAP Q3 ■ Bisazza Street

A wide variety of books on Malta, as well as works for children, fiction and non-fiction titles, are available in this useful bookstore, which is spread over two floors.

6 Gadget Gadget, Sliema
MAP Q3 ■ 2a Triq San Duminku

An ideal place to find unique pieces of decor for the house, Gadget Gadget also sells a range of cards and interesting gift options.

7 Bisazza Street, Sliema
MAP Q3

Serious shoppers visiting Sliema should not overlook this avenue. As well as the Plaza Shopping Centre and a supermarket, all the usual premium chains can be found on or around Bisazza Street, including Next, Mango and dozens more.

8 Pedigree Toyshops, St Julian's
MAP N1 ■ Bay Street Tourist Complex, Level 0, St George's Bay

This branch of one of Malta's top toy retailers has all you need to keep young kids happy indoors, on the beach, or on the plane. It's also a good back-up on a rainy day.

9 Diamonds International, St Julian's
MAP N1 ■ Portomaso

Choose from diamonds, pearls, gold, silver and a plethora of other options offered at Diamonds International, Malta's largest jewellery shop.

10 Tower Stores, Sliema
MAP Q3 ■ Triq Il-Kbira

Malta's fruit-and-vegetable vans and village shops supply most visitors' needs, but there are occasions when a supermarket comes in handy. There are now many in Malta to choose from, but Tower Stores is the biggest in this area and you should find everything you want here.

Nightlife

The amazing view across the bay looking out from Twenty Two

1 **Twenty Two, St Julian's**
MAP N1 ■ Portomaso

A sophisticated bar frequented by an international crowd, Twenty Two occupies a spectacular location on the top floor of the Portomaso Tower.

2 **Dragonara Palace Casino, St Julian's**
MAP E3 ■ Dragonara Point

This 19th-century palazzo by the sea is Malta's most lavish casino, with gaming tables, slot machines and live entertainment. Dress smartly and take ID. It's for over-18s only.

3 **Places Club, Paceville**
MAP N1 ■ Ball Street

Popular with the younger set, this club has a great party ambience and holds special events on Friday nights. Great offers at the bar pull in a big crowd. Commercial house is played more than any other genre of music.

4 **The Scotsman Pub, Paceville**
MAP N1 ■ Triq San Ġorġ

Serving traditional British pub fare, the cosy, tartan-filled Scotsman offers a great selection of spirits and draught beers to fuel its lively Karaoke nights.

5 **Havana Club, Paceville**
MAP D3 ■ Triq San Ġorġ

One of the best clubs for R&B, soul and hip-hop on the island, situated right in the heart of Paceville.

6 **Juuls, St Julian's**
MAP N1 ■ 57 Triq San Ġiljan, Spinola Bay

A characterful, cosy reggae club serving cocktails and fresh fruit juices and playing the best reggae, roots, dub and ragga on the islands.

7 **Hugo's Passion, Paceville**
MAP N1 ■ Triq San Ġorġ

In the centre of Paceville, this club sits atop the popular Hugo's Lounge. Let out your inner party animal on the dance floor, then unwind in the sofa lounge or at the outdoor tables.

8 **Qube, Paceville**
MAP N1 ■ Triq Santa Rita

Open till 4am daily, this vodka-themed bar has 60 brands and offers myriad flavours. Special promotions are held here on Wednesdays.

9 **Eden SuperBowl and Cinemas, St Julian's**
MAP N1 ■ Triq San Ġorġ ■ Adm

This is Malta's biggest cinema complex-cum-bowling alley with 16 screens, plus an IMAX cinema.

10 **Portomaso Casino, St Julian's**
MAP N1 ■ Portomaso

Set below the Portomaso Tower, this casino offers classic games like blackjack and roulette, alongside slot machines. It also has the largest poker room in Malta.

See map on p72 ←

Bars and Cafés

A typical healthy dish on the menu at Mint

① Mint, Sliema
MAP Q2 ■ Triq Windsor

With the emphasis put on fresh and healthy food, this family-friendly café offers a variety of options catering for vegetarians and people with special dietary needs. Orders are taken at the counter before taking a seat.

② Marina Terrace, St Julian's
MAP N1 ■ Portomaso

Enjoy a brunch, lunch or an afternoon snack at this pizzeria and brasserie overlooking the pretty Portomaso Marina. A wide variety of wraps, burgers and sandwiches are served here. Outdoor seating is available and there is also free Wi-Fi.

③ Cara's Café, Sliema
MAP P2 ■ 249 Triq It-Torri

Popular with tourists and locals alike, this bustling café has a great location on Sliema's seafront promenade. It serves snacks and light meals, but the cakes are the highlight.

④ Vinotheque Wine & Cheese Bar, St Julian's
MAP D3 ■ Corinthia Marina Hotel, St George's Bay

This bright and breezy wine bar in a smart hotel offers an excellent array of local and overseas wines, which are accompanied by light meals and snacks. There's a pleasant terrace for relaxing in summer.

⑤ Dubliners, St Julian's
MAP N1 ■ Spinola Bay

Expatriates and locals alike enjoy a delicious Sunday roast at this cosy Irish-themed bar that serves draught beers, wines and spirits. It also hosts live music programmes regularly.

⑥ Hole in the Wall, Sliema
MAP Q3 ■ 31 High Street

Once a horse stable, this neighbourhood hangout has been around for nearly a century, making it the oldest bar in Sliema. There are live music performances in the small loft space.

⑦ Café Cuba, Sliema
MAP Q3 ■ Triq ix-Xatt

Frequented by the shopping crowd, this seafront café is a great place to chill out. It offers a variety of wines, beers and cocktails and the burgers served here are extremely popular.

⑧ Del Borgo Wine Bar, Birgu
MAP L5 ■ Triq San Duminku

This lively bar boasts an excellent and extensive wine list and a menu of local delicacies. A major highlight is the tasty Maltese bread pudding.

⑨ Café Giorgio, Sliema
MAP Q3 ■ Triq Ix-Xatt

On Sliema's seafront, Café Giorgia is the perfect people-watching spot. Soak up the evening sun on the terrace while watching the Maltese stroll past during their *passeggiata*.

⑩ The Jazz Cave, St Julian's
MAP N1 ■ Hotel Juliani, Spinola Bay

Malta's jazz hot spot is Art Deco in design and has a laid-back atmosphere. Patrons enjoy fine dining paired with nightly live music by local and international artists.

See map on p72

Restaurants

1 Barracuda, St Julian's
MAP N2 ■ 194 Triq Il-Kbira,
Balluta Bay ■ 2133 1817 ■ €€€
Set in a villa leaning out over the water, this elegant and romantic restaurant is well known for its superb seafood and flavourful Mediterranean cuisine.

2 Tal-Petut, Birgu
MAP L5 ■ 20 Triq P. Scicluna
■ 7942 1169 ■ €€
Chef Donald creates a private dining experience at Tal-Petut by formulating a separate menu for each customer. Advance reservations are necessary.

3 The Avenue, Paceville
MAP N1 ■ Triq Gort ■ 2135
1753 ■ €
Kids love this very popular restaurant, which is brightly decorated in bold colours. It serves great pizzas and pasta at bargain prices. Book in advance or be prepared to queue.

4 Villa Brasserie, St Julian's
MAP N2 ■ 39 Triq Il-Kbira, Balluta Bay
■ 7945 1513 ■ €€
Set in a 19th-century seaside palazzo and with impressive water views from the terrace, this brasserie offers a varied and creative á la carte menu.

5 Zest, St Julian's
MAP N1 ■ 25 Triq San Ġorġ
■ 2138 7600 ■ Closed Sun ■ €€
This chic restaurant offers modern continental and Asian food. Enjoy a pre-dinner drink on the terrace.

Stylish decor with pink accents at Zest

PRICE CATEGORIES
For a three-course meal for one with half a bottle of wine (or equivalent meal), taxes and extra charges.

€ under €30   €€ €30–€50   €€€ over €50

6 Raffael, St Julian's
MAP N1 ■ Spinola Bay
■ 2135 2000 ■ €
Overlooking Spinola Bay, Raffael offers great salads, freshly prepared pizzas, homemade burgers, Maltese classics and traditional English breakfast.

7 Sottovento, Birgu
MAP K5 ■ Vittoriosa Waterfront
■ 2180 8990 ■ €€
On the way to Fort St Angelo, this place specializes in Mediterranean cuisine, fish and stone-baked pizza.

8 Cucina del-Sole, Sliema
MAP Q2 ■ Tigne Point ■ 2060
3434 ■ €€
This unassuming eatery, overlooking the Valletta bastions, serves Mediterranean food.

9 Peppino's, St Julian's
MAP N1 ■ 31 Triq San Ġorġ
■ 2137 3200 ■ Closed Sun ■ €€
Brick walls, French windows and an Italian menu set the tone of this restaurant with its waterfront views.

10 Blue Elephant, St Julian's
MAP N1 ■ Hilton Hotel,
Portomaso ■ 2138 3383 ■ Closed D
daily ■ €€
The finest Thai cuisine in Malta; dine on the terrace overlooking the marina, or inside in rainforest decor.

🔟 Northern Malta

Northern Malta has an unusually diverse range of attractions. Some of the island's boldest and brashest resorts can be found here – in particular the summer party capital of Buġibba. St Paul's Bay and the resort of Mellieħa are somewhat quieter and the golden sands at Mellieħa Bay are the most popular on the island. If the kids get bored of the sun, sea and sand, note that Malta's top family attractions are here – from water parks to the Popeye Village film set.

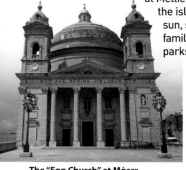

Then there's a wilder side of Malta: stunning cliff walks, extraordinary coastal scenery and remote coves, especially around Marfa Ridge. For wild Malta of a different kind, visit the Għadira Nature Reserve. Finally, there's ancient Malta, seen in the Skorba and Ta Ħaġrat Temples.

The "Egg Church" at Mġarr

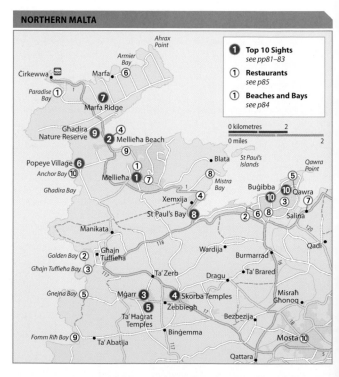

NORTHERN MALTA

Ahrax Point

Armier Bay

Ċirkewwa

Marfa **6**

Paradise Bay **1**

7 Marfa Ridge

Għadira Nature Reserve **9** **4** **2** Mellieħa Beach **9**

Popeye Village **6**
Anchor Bay **10**

Mellieħa **1** **1** **7**

Ghadira Bay

Blata

Xemxija **4**

St Paul's Islands

Qawra Point

8 Mistra Bay

Buġibba **10** **10** Qawra **5**

2 **6** **8** Salina **3** **7**

St Paul's Bay **8**

Manikata

Wardija

Burmarrad

Qadi

Golden Bay **2** Għajn Tuffieħa

Għajn Tuffieħa Bay **3**

Ta' Zerb

Dragu

Ta' Brared

Gnejna Bay **5** Mġarr **3** **4** Skorba Temples

Żebbiegħ

Misraħ Għonoq

Ta' Ħaġrat Temples **5**

Bezbezija

Fomm Riħ Bay **9** Ta' Abatija

Binġemma

Mosta **10**

Qattara

1	**Top 10 Sights** see pp81–83
1	**Restaurants** see p85
1	**Beaches and Bays** see p84

0 kilometres   2

0 miles   2

The parish church of Mellieħa

1 Mellieħa
MAP B2

The historic town of Mellieħa sits high above the bay and beach. Although Mellieħa was one of the first parishes in Malta, the original 15th-century settlement proved too hard to defend from pirates and was largely abandoned until the 19th century. Mellieħa has a church from each period – the oldest is venerated for a rock painting that legend attributed to St Luke.

2 Mellieħa Beach
MAP B2

The longest beach in Malta. Mellieħa is perfect for families, with its sandy shallows shelving gently. It's a pity about the main road that runs the length of the bay, but the golden yellow sand and clear sea are superb and there are lots of facilities: cafés, watersports, banana rides and paragliding. Resort hotels dominate either end of the beach, while there is also accommodation in the village up the hill.

3 Mġarr
MAP B3

There are two places called Mġarr in the Maltese islands: the harbour in Gozo and this sleepy little village on the island of Malta. The locals' pride and joy is the "Egg Church", built in the 1930s with funds raised by the sale of eggs. You can also explore an underground shelter used during World War II; the rooms have been refurbished to look as they would have during the bombardment of Malta. Mġarr is a good place to try the Maltese dish of *fenek*, or rabbit *(see p56)*, cooked in various ways.

4 Skorba Temples, Żebbiegħ
MAP B3 ■ Near Mġarr ■ 2158 0590
■ Open 9am–4:30pm Tue, Thu, Sat
■ Adm ■ www.heritagemalta.org

The Skorba Temples are believed to be among the oldest free-standing structures in the world. The site has provided significant information for archaeologists but there is little to see *(see p43)*. Look out for holes cut into the paving slabs at the entrance; it has been suggested that the blood of sacrificed animals was poured in the holes to propitiate the gods.

5 Ta' Ħaġrat Temples, Mġarr
MAP B4 ■ Triq San Pietru ■ 2158 6264
■ Open 9am–4:30pm Tue, Thu, Sat
■ Adm ■ www.heritagemalta.org

These temples *(see p42)* were first excavated in the 1920s under the direction of the Maltese scholar Sir Themistocles Zammit.

Ruins of the Ta' Ħaġrat temples

Popeye Village, set around the fictional seaside town of Sweethaven

6 Popeye Village, Anchor Bay

MAP A3 ▪ 2152 4782 ▪ Open 9:30am–7pm daily ▪ Adm ▪ www.popeyemalta.com

Anchor Bay was named after the scores of stone Roman anchors that washed up there. Since 1980, it has been known for a Hollywood film set – the Popeye Village. Wander the wackily wonky streets of Popeye's hometown, Sweethaven *(see p54)*.

7 Marfa Ridge
MAP B2

On a map, the Marfa Ridge looks like a fish's tail tacked onto the round

Colossal cliffs at the Marfa Ridge

body of the island. The most notable landmarks are the storybook crenellations of the Red Tower and the towering cliffs of Ras Il-Qammieh. The impressive coastline is pitted with numerous coves and beaches, and the whole area is a paradise for walkers *(see p48)*.

8 St Paul's Bay
MAP B3

St Paul's is the prettiest of the clutch of resorts that line the shores around the bay of the same name. St Paul's Bay retains some vestiges of the salty old fishing cove from which it developed: its small port, with its fleet of brightly painted *luzzus*, is still utterly charming. It has no beaches, but there are some stretches of flat rocks on which to sunbathe.

ST PAUL IN MALTA

According to legend, St Paul was shipwrecked in AD 60 in the bay now known as St Paul's Bay. He was attacked by a poisonous viper but, to the astonishment of the local people, survived completely unhurt (a waspish Maltese saying suggests that when the venom left Malta's vipers, it entered the tongues of Maltese women). St Paul went on to convert the Roman governor Publius to Christianity, and appointed him first bishop of Malta.

9 **Għadira Nature Reserve**
MAP B2 ■ Għadira, Mellieħa Bay
■ 2134 7646 ■ Open Nov–May:
10:30am–4:30pm Sat–Sun ■ www.
birdlifemalta.org

The illegal hunting and trapping of birds in Malta *(see p110)* has long caused international outrage. This nature reserve, set just behind the sandy beach at Mellieħa, was established as a haven for migrating birds by BirdLife, the local chapter of an international conservation group. Having gained considerable support from the locals, they opened a second reserve near Xemxija. Open and family days are regularly organized; volunteers conduct guided tours at weekends and on other days visits can be arranged by appointment. In Malta, more than almost anywhere else, migration dominates the ornithological year, so the birds you observe at this reserve will depend on the season.

Buġibba as it lights up after dark

10 **Buġibba and Qawra**
MAP C3

Big, brash Buġibba and its quieter neighbour Qawra are two of the islands' largest resort areas. Both are geared towards the package tourism market; in summer, most of the hotels are block-booked by tour operators. Buġibba has the greatest concentration of nightlife, so you might get a better night's sleep in Qawra. Life in Buġibba centres on the cobbled main square and the elevated man-made beach. Both areas offer lidos, boat trips and watersports. It can be hard to get around without a car, but you can take excursions.

A DRIVE AROUND NORTHERN MALTA

MORNING

This trip starts in **Mellieħa** *(see p81)*. Begin with a morning dip at **Mellieħa Beach** *(see p81)*. If the little **Għadira Nature Reserve** is open, drop in for a bird tour, especially if it's the spring or autumn migratory season. If you are travelling with kids, head west to **Popeye Village** for an enjoyable tour around the old film set before taking the main road from Mellieħa up to the **Marfa Ridge**. Stop by the **Red Tower** for a bit of Knights' history and panoramic views over Comino and Gozo before continuing out to **Ras Il-Qammieħ** to see the spectacular cliffs. Head back towards Mellieħa and up into the village for a look around the historic churches and lunch in one of the restaurants.

AFTERNOON

Drive south to **St Paul's Bay** (where the saint is said to have been shipwrecked) and then follow the road for 4 km (2 miles) through the fertile **Pwales Valley**, with its green fields girdled by tumbling stone walls. Park at the top of the cliff and make the descent via almost 200 stone steps to **Għajn Tuffieħa Bay** *(see p84)*. Work on your tan for a couple of hours or, if you are feeling more active, you could hike around the headland to the busier beach at **Golden Bay** *(see p84)*, or perhaps take a boat trip to the quiet cove at **Fomm Ir-Riħ** *(see p84)*. The little village of **Mġarr** *(see p81)* is famous for its old-fashioned Maltese cooking. Alternatively, head back to St Paul's Bay and enjoy a drink at the bayside **Gillieru** *(see p85)*.

See map on p80 ←

Beaches and Bays

① Paradise Bay
MAP A2

This snug bay, with a crescent of sand reached by a flight of steps cut into the rock, is a very popular spot – it is best visited during the week or out of season.

② Ġnejna Bay
MAP A3

This is a picturesque bay with a small stretch of sand in the middle of a wide arc of flat rocks, backed by creamy limestone cliffs. A handful of boathouses overlooks tiny coves. It's a favourite with local families.

③ Golden Bay
MAP A3

This popular sandy beach is easily accessible and offers good amenities including canoe and pedalo rental. The beach is subject to dangerous currents from time to time; don't swim if the red flag is flying.

④ Mellieħa Beach
This narrow shoreline is Malta's largest sandy beach. It is easy to reach by bus or car and has excellent amenities, making it very popular with families (see p81).

⑤ Għajn Tuffieħa Bay
MAP A3

A beautiful bay set against terraced hills, Għajn Tuffieħa has lovely cliff walks stretching off in either direction.

⑥ Little Armier
MAP B2

Beaches Armier and Little Armier are side by side. The first is scruffy and rather unappealing, but the latter is a sandy little cove with a beach café.

⑦ Salina Bay
MAP C3

The broad sweep of Salina Bay is lined with hotels and apartment blocks. There is no beach as such, but the flat rocks are good for sunbathing, and the shallow waters perfect for a dip.

⑧ Mistra Bay
MAP B3

It's easy to miss the turning for this delightful little strand near Xemxija: a country road scented with honey-suckle leads to the narrow bay where the swimming and snorkelling are good and relatively undisturbed.

⑨ Fomm Ir-Riħ Bay
MAP A4

This wild and beautiful beach is hard to get to so few people make it here, except in the height of summer.

⑩ Anchor Bay
MAP A3

This pretty little cove next to the touristy Popeye Village (see p82) somehow gets overlooked by the crowds. The sandy beach is little and compact, but it's a good spot for a picnic.

The sandy beach at Għajn Tuffieħa Bay

Restaurants

1 The Arches, Mellieħa
MAP B3 ▪ 113 Triq Gorg Borg Olivier ▪ 7999 5611 ▪ Closed Sun & Mon ▪ €€

Lovely and light-filled, with a small covered terrace, the Arches serves some of Malta's best French cuisine. The service and wine list are excellent.

2 Gillieru, St Paul's Bay
MAP B3 ▪ 66 Triq Il-Knisja ▪ 2157 3480 ▪ €€

A large, family-friendly place with a perfect setting overlooking the bay, Gillieru is good for lunch, dinner or a coffee break. Try the ultra-fresh fish.

Gillieru, sitting directly on St Paul's Bay

3 La Krepree, Buġibba
MAP C3 ▪ 165 Dawret Il-Gzejjer ▪ 2157 1517 ▪ Closed L, Sun ▪ €

Come for French-style crêpes – both sweet and savoury – while enjoying the lively seafront views from the terrace outside.

4 Zeus, St Paul's Bay
MAP B3 ▪ Xemxija Hill ▪ 2157 8585 ▪ Closed Mon, Jul & Aug ▪ €

With a range of classic and authentic Greek dishes on offer, this family-run restaurant is a favourite with locals.

5 Lovage Bistro, Buġibba
MAP C3 ▪ Triq l-Imħar, St Paul's Bay ▪ 2157 2088 ▪ Closed Tue ▪ €

This cosy bistro offers a creative menu that combines home-grown style with a modern twist. There's patio seating with a bar during the warmer months.

PRICE CATEGORIES

For a three-course meal for one with half a bottle of wine (or equivalent meal), taxes and extra charges.

€ under €30 €€ €30–€50 €€€ over €50

6 Tarragon, St Paul's Bay
MAP B3 ▪ 21 Church Street ▪ 2157 3759 ▪ Closed L Mon–Sat ▪ €€

Famous for its out-of-this-world daily specials, the wine list here is stellar and the staff knowledgeable.

7 Il-Mithna, Mellieħa
MAP B3 ▪ 58 Triq Il-Kbira ▪ 2152 0404 ▪ Closed Sun ▪ €€

Innovative fusion food is served with a Maltese twist at this restaurant that was originally a 17th-century mill.

8 SALT – Kitchen & Lounge, Buġibba
MAP C3 ▪ Triq Il-Korp Tal-Pijunieri ▪ 2157 8004 ▪ €

SALT's chef and owner is dedicated to sustainability, serving fresh, Mediterranean dishes using locally ingredients. There is also an impressive wine list.

9 Xatba, Mellieħa
MAP B2 ▪ Triq Il-Marfa ▪ 2152 1753 ▪ Closed L daily ▪ €

Rich pasta and risotto dishes, perfectly prepared fresh fish and grilled meats are served at this family-run restaurant, a favourite with locals and tourists.

10 Ta'Marija Restaurant, Mosta
MAP C4 ▪ Constitution Street ▪ 2143 4444 ▪ Closed Mon L ▪ €€

Family-run since 1964, Ta'Marija celebrates Maltese food and culture. Their folklore-themed dinners, with traditional dance and music, are legendary with locals and tourists.

See map on p80 ←

🔟 Central Malta

Poised on a plateau in the very centre of the island, behind impenetrable walls, Mdina is Malta's ancient capital and its most beautiful city. Its streets are charged with history, and, particularly after dusk, each faded palace and medieval chapel seems to whisper its secrets. Nearby Rabat is just as old and has a special place in the hearts of the devout Maltese: it was here that St Paul was supposedly brought after the shipwreck in AD 60. To the south, the gorgeous Dingli Cliffs are perfect for hiking and picnicking, with fine views, while the shady Buskett Gardens offer respite from the summer heat, and the cart ruts of "Clapham Junction" remain mysterious. Mosta, one of the largest towns on the island, is dominated – as is much of the island – by the enormous dome of its parish church, which miraculously escaped destruction during World War II.

Statue of St Mary at Attard church

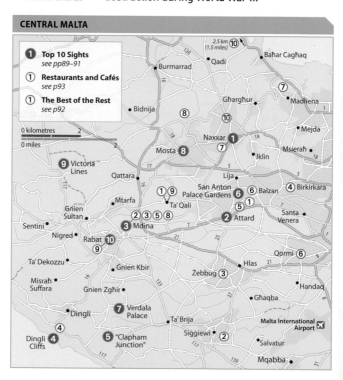

CENTRAL MALTA

1 **Top 10 Sights**
see pp89–91

1 **Restaurants and Cafés**
see p93

1 **The Best of the Rest**
see p92

Previous pages Beneath the Mosta Dome, Church of Our Lady of the Assumption

The Music (or Gold Room) at Palazzo Parisio

1 Palazzo Parisio, Naxxar

MAP C4 ■ Pjazza Vittorja ■
2141 2461 ■ Open 9am–5:30pm daily
■ Adm ■ www.palazzoparisio.com

This aristocratic palace was built for
the popular Portuguese Grand Master
Manoel de Vilhena *(see p46)* in 1733.
At the end of the 19th century, it was
bought by Scicluna, a noble philan-
thropist, who transformed it into the
present-day opulent and fashionable
mansion with a gilded ballroom.
Don't miss the beautiful formal
Baroque gardens – part of the
famous Grandi Giardini Italiani
Collection – elegant and particularly
lovely in spring.

2 The Three Villages (Balzan, Lija, Attard)

MAP C4, D4

These villages consist of three
neighbouring settlements. At first
glance, they blend blandly into the
suburban sprawl that extends dustily
over much of Malta. And yet their
historic kernels contain some of the
island's most desirable addresses.
Safe from the Ottomans after the
Great Siege of 1565, the Maltese
began a building boom, and the
smartest villas and palaces were
built in the Three Villages. The
villages grew, and their boundaries
merged, but they remained fashionable under the British and even

today. A wander through
these affluent streets
brings you face to face
with medieval parish
churches and Baroque
villas, English-style
mansions and contem-
porary luxury apartment
blocks. The loveliest
church is the parish
church at Attard, built
in 1613 by Tommaso
Dingli and probably the
finest Renaissance
church on the islands.

3 Mdina

Time stopped
for this ancient capital
when the seafaring
Knights arrived in the 1530s, settling
around the Grand Harbour – and
sidelining Mdina and its people in the
process. "The Silent City", as it is still
known, may fill up with tourists by
day, but the hush returns with nightfall
when the crowds depart. If you can,
explore this lovely city by day, and
again by night *(see pp20–21)*.

4 Dingli Cliffs

MAP B5

The spectacular Dingli Cliffs are wild
and undeveloped – a rare treat on
the crowded little island of Malta
(see p49). They provide the perfect
terrain for walking and picnics, with
fine views out to little Filfla Island.

Dingli Cliffs plunging into the sea

5 "Clapham Junction"
MAP C5 ■ Dingli Cliffs, near Buskett Gardens ■ 24-hour access ■ www.heritagemalta.org

This dramatic site of mysterious pairs of grooves etched in the rocks on a wild and beautiful plateau is likely to have been formed by vehicles carrying stone from nearby quarries in Classical times (see p42).

Pond at San Anton Palace Gardens

6 San Anton Palace Gardens, Attard
MAP C4 ■ De G Portelli ■ Open 7am–6pm daily

These quiet and beautiful gardens are tucked away in San Anton, a suburb of Attard. The gardens are attached to a splendid summer palace, built by Grand Master Antoine de Paule in the 1620s. The palace (closed to visitors) is now the official residence of the president of Malta, but a section of the palace gardens has been open to the public since 1882. They are at their best in spring, when the manicured flowerbeds and elegantly arranged flowerpots explode in a riot of colour. A small aviary contains exotic birds.

THE MIRACLE AT MOSTA

A congregation of about 300 people had gathered for Mass on the afternoon of 9 April 1942 when a German bomb pierced the lofty Mosta Dome, clattered onto the floor and skidded through the church. Unbelievably, the bomb didn't explode, and the Maltese have always chosen to interpret this as a miracle. You can see a replica of the bomb, along with some period photographs of the church during World War II, in a small museum that is part of the church.

---

7 Verdala Palace and Buskett Gardens
MAP C5 ■ Triq Il-Buskett

Visible from much of southern Malta, the crenellated turrets of Verdala Palace seem to float above dense forest. The palace (not open to the public) was built as a summer residence for Grand Master Hughes de Verdalle in 1588, but it is now the official residence of the Maltese president. The forest, known as the Buskett Gardens (see p49), is Malta's only real woodlands, with leafy paths and picnic areas.

8 Mosta Dome, Mosta
MAP C4 ■ Pjazza Rotunda ■ 2143 3826 ■ Open 9–11am, 3–5pm Mon–Sat

The gigantic dome of Mosta's parish church is visible from much of the island. Once the third-largest dome in Europe, it was relegated to fourth place in 1971 when the Xewkija

Beneath the magnificent Mosta Dome

Rotunda (see p102) in Gozo was completed – at least according to the Gozitans. The people of Mosta are insistent that their dome beats that of Xewkija when measured by width rather than by height (see p45).

9 Victoria Lines
MAP B4

The Victoria Lines, 12 km (7 miles) of fortification stretching right across the width of Malta, were built by the British towards the end of the 19th century. The idea was to prevent invasion overland by invaders dropping anchor in the north of the island. The defensive wall, built along a natural ridge (the Great Fault) links three forts – one at each end and the Mosta Fort in the middle. Obsolete within a few years of its completion in 1897, the walkway along the top of the wall makes for a great hike with panoramic views.

Mosaic at the Domus Romana in Rabat

10 Rabat
MAP C4

Mdina and Rabat were once a single entity, before the Arabs walled and fortified Mdina almost a thousand years ago. Rabat retains the islands' most evocative Roman remains in its Domus Romana. The remnants of this once opulent Roman villa are beside a museum containing mosaics and frescoes from the Roman era. Many of Malta's most resonant religious sites are concentrated in Rabat, including the grotto where St Paul is said to have lived after he was shipwrecked, catacombs dating to the early years of Christianity, and a cave painted with 14th-century murals where St Agatha is said to have hidden (see pp20–21).

A WALK IN MDINA

▶ MORNING

Enter Mdina (see pp20–21) through the **main gate**. Almost immediately on the right, you'll pass the **Palazzo Vilhena** (now the Natural History Museum). Peek at the patio by the main entrance (the museum is not particularly large) before heading to the sumptuous **Xara Palace Hotel** (see p115) for coffee in its 18th-century palazzo. Continue up narrow Triq San Pawl until you reach **St Paul's Cathedral**, one of the most beautiful ecclesiastical buildings in Malta. Across the square, the **Cathedral Museum** is an enjoyably chaotic treasure-trove of unexpected delights. The highlight is the collection of magnificent Dürer engravings and woodcuts. Now is a good time for lunch; try one of the cafés behind St Paul's Square.

AFTERNOON

Walk up **Triq Villegaignon**, Mdina's finest street, lined with elaborate churches and graceful palaces with worn stone escutcheons. Look out for the **Casa Testaferrata** on the right; the French governor was thrown from the balcony of this noble house in 1798, when the Maltese decided they had had enough of the greedy French troops. Farther up, the **Palazzo Falson** is the best-preserved medieval palace in Mdina. Triq Villegaignon soon opens up into the **Pjazza Tas-Sur** (Bastion Square), where breath-taking views of the whole of central Malta unfold. Close by, the pretty open-air **Fontanella Tea Gardens** (see p93) is a good stop for cake and impressive views.

See map on p88 ←

The Best of the Rest

Air Battle Hanger, Aviation Museum

1 Malta Aviation Museum

MAP C4 ■ Ta' Qali Airfield, between Mdina and Attard ■ Open 9am–5pm daily ■ Adm ■ www. maltaaviationmuseum.com

This fascinating museum showcases an extensive collection of vintage aircraft, including a WWII Spitfire and a Hawker Hurricane *(see p54)*.

2 Limestone Heritage, Siġġiewi

MAP C5 ■ Triq Mons M Azzopardi ■ 2146 4931 ■ Open 9am–4pm Mon–Fri, 9–11:30am Sat ■ Adm ■ www. limestoneheritage.com

Malta is one huge quarry, the source of the stone that built the ancient temples and the city of Valletta. Audiovisual displays at this former quarry tell the story.

3 Żebbuġ

MAP C5

A tattered triumphal arch hints at Żebbuġ's former glory. Its vast church, designed by Gerolamo Cassar, architect of St John's, Valletta, has fared better, and its elegant spires float above the town.

Glass produced at Ta' Qali Crafts Village

4 Birkirkara

MAP D4

One of the largest Maltese towns since medieval times, Birkirkara preserves a small and atmospheric old quarter and a fine Baroque church famous for its large bell.

5 Wignacourt Aqueduct, Attard

MAP C4 ■ Triq Peter Paul Rubens

This 16-km (10-mile) aqueduct funded in 1610 by Grand Master Wignacourt was still bringing water from Rabat to Valletta more than two centuries later.

6 Qormi

MAP D4

An otherwise humdrum town, Qormi has two claims to fame: it makes the best bread in the islands, and it has one of the most flamboyant Baroque churches, the Church of St George.

7 Fort Madliena

MAP D3 ■ 7928 3383 ■ Open Sat for tours by appointment

This sturdy, pentagonal fort was one of four built to defend the Victoria Lines. Fort Madliena still commands the surrounding countryside from its lofty promontory. Best of all are the views out over the fortified walls, which spill down a steep gorge.

8 Fort Mosta

MAP C3 ■ Open Mon for tours

One of four British-built forts that guarded the Victoria Lines, this well-preserved example of Victorian engineering was finished in 1879 but never saw battle.

9 Ta' Qali Crafts Village

MAP C4 ■ Ta' Qali Crafts Village, between Mdina and Attard ■ Open 9am–4pm Mon–Fri; 9am–noon Sat

Nissen set at a former RAF airfield with traditional Maltese crafts, from glass-blowing to pottery.

10 San Pawl Tat-Tarġa

MAP C3 ■ Naxxar

St Paul is said to have preached from here – hence the chapel. There are also 16th-century towers, a World War II pillbox and some of Malta's mysterious ancient cart ruts.

Restaurants and Cafés

PRICE CATEGORIES

For a three-course meal for one with half a bottle of wine (or equivalent meal), taxes and extra charges.

€ under €30 €€ €30–€50 €€€ over €50

① Rickshaw, Balzan

MAP D4 ▪ Corinthia Palace Hotel, De Paule Ave, Balzan ▪ 2144 0301 ▪ Closed Sun, Mon & L ▪ €€€

One of Malta's best Far Eastern restaurants, Rickshaw serves good Oriental cocktails and has an impressive menu to match.

② de Mondion, Mdina

MAP C4 ▪ Xara Palace Hotel ▪ 2145 0560 ▪ Closed L daily ▪ €€€

One of Malta's few genuine foodie temples, de Mondion is located in one of its most beautiful hotels, the Xara Palace (see p115). Come here to eat superb food in a romantic setting.

③ Trattoria AD 1530, Mdina

MAP C4 ▪ Xara Palace Hotel ▪ 2145 0560 ▪ €€

An array of pizza, pasta and salads are served throughout the day at this relaxed trattoria set on a lovely patio.

④ The Cliffs

MAP B5 ▪ Triq Panoramika Dingli ▪ 2145 5470 ▪ Closed Tue ▪ €

Standing on the top of Dingli Cliffs, this is both a restaurant and an interpretation centre. The menu celebrates the natural landscape – seasonal produce is used, and salads are made with native plants.

⑤ Medina, Mdina

MAP C4 ▪ 7 Triq Is-Salib Imqaddes ▪ 2145 4004 ▪ Closed Sun ▪ €€

Medina's thick stone walls have stood here for almost a thousand years. In summer, you can dine under vines outside in the courtyard. The menu beautifully fuses French, Italian and Mediterranean cuisines.

⑥ Fra Giuseppe's, Balzan

MAP D4 ▪ 3 Triq Dun Spir Sammut, Balzan ▪ 2149 9440 ▪ €

Set in a former doctor's surgery, this wine bar has traditional Maltese fare. In summer, tables are set up outside.

⑦ Caffé Luna, Naxxar

MAP D4 ▪ Palazzo Parisio & Gardens ▪ 2141 2461 ▪ Closed Mon–Wed D ▪ €€

With stylish interiors and a canopied terrace garden, this is a favourite meeting place for a light lunch or traditional afternoon tea.

Terrace at the Fontanella Tea Gardens

⑧ Fontanella Tea Gardens, Mdina

MAP C4 ▪ 1 Bastion Street ▪ 2145 4264 ▪ €

Perched on the ramparts, Fontanella has spectacular views. The cakes are famous across Malta, and served in an ivy-clad courtyard or out on the terrace. Service can be a little slow.

⑨ L'Agape, Rabat

MAP C4 ▪ 25 Triq San Kataldu ▪ 2099 2209 ▪ Closed Sun ▪ €

L'Agape uses fresh, seasonal ingredients and has a menu that changes daily.

⑩ Giuseppi's Bar & Bistro, Naxxar

MAP D4 ▪ Salini Resort, Salini Bay ▪ 2157 4882 ▪ Closed Sun ▪ €€€

Here, traditional dishes are given a modern twist. The rabbit with bitter chocolate sauce is popular with locals.

See map on p88

TOP 10 Southern Malta

This southern corner of the island is rural and tranquil, with patchwork fields defined by old stone walls. Each little village has its own ornate Baroque church at the centre of village life, and is best seen when lit up for the *festa*. The region boasts the island's two most picturesque temples, the loveliest medieval chapels and the most exceptional ancient site in the necropolis of the Ħal Saflieni Hypogeum, as well as the prettiest fishing harbour at Marsaxlokk.

Pretty Marsaxlokk harbour

SOUTHERN MALTA

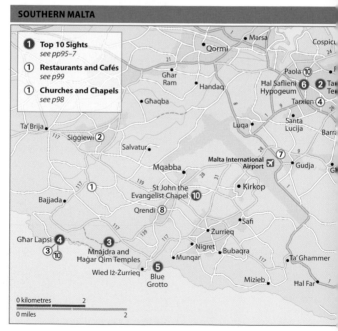

1 **Top 10 Sights**
see pp95–7

1 **Restaurants and Cafés**
see p99

1 **Churches and Chapels**
see p98

1 Għar Dalam Cave and Museum, Birżebbuġa

MAP E6 ■ Triq Għar Dalam ■ 2165 7419 ■ Open 9am–4:30pm daily ■ Adm ■ www.heritagemalta.org

Għar Dalam is a unique cave and prehistoric site, where a spectacular collection of 180,000-year-old bones belonging to long-extinct animals was deposited at the end of the Ice Age *(see p43)*. There is a small museum attached, where two rooms display the main finds of the palaeontologists.

2 Tarxien Temples

MAP E5 ■ Triq It-Tempji Neolitiċi ■ 2169 5578 ■ Open daily 9am–4:30pm ■ Adm ■ www.heritagemalta.org

The Tarxien Temples are the most complex of Malta's temple sites, and include a cremation cemetery that was in use before the Bronze Age.

Bronze Age artifact from Tarxien

Extensive prehistoric art and decorative objects have been found here, including part of a colossal human figure and beautiful spiral and animal reliefs *(see p42)*.

3 Mnajdra and Ħaġar Qim Temples

These two temples emerge from a blanket of poppies on a clifftop overlooking the sea. Overgrown fields with limestone walls stretch in every direction, and the lonely location only adds to the atmosphere. The temples are made of soft limestone, which wind and time have eroded into lacy shapes. Both temples are fascinating; Ħaġar Qim is the largest and most complex, while Mnajdra seems to have been designed to act as a stone calendar *(see pp18–19)*.

4 Għar Lapsi

MAP C6

A natural lido formed by a rock pool scooped from the cliff, Għar Lapsi sounds much prettier than it is. The setting is attractive enough, but the pools are coated with seaweed and surrounded by unappealing buildings. In spite of this, the Maltese come in droves during the summer months. Watching the comings and goings of the fishermen who use the cove is a pleasant way to spend an afternoon. A couple of restaurants with good views overlook the lido.

Rocky coast around Għar Lapsi

5 Blue Grotto, Wied Iż-Żurrieq

MAP D6 ■ Boats depart from Wied Iż-Żurrieq about every 15 mins, 9am–4:30pm (7pm in high season) daily

At the tiny cove a straggle of café-bars and shops have sprung up to cater for the streams of visitors on their way to see the fabled Blue Grotto. Walk along the cliff path or take a boat ride into the massive cave *(see p49)*.

Blue Grotto seen from the cliff path

6 Ħal Saflieni Hypogeum

Malta's most amazing ancient treasure, this vast 5,000-year-old underground cemetery was hewn by hand from the rock. It was here that the famous sculpture of the "Sleeping Lady" *(see p28)* was found. If you see only one prehistoric site in Malta, make it this one – but be sure to book well ahead *(see pp28–9)*.

THE NOT-SO-GREAT WHITE SHARK

Little Wied Iż-Żurrieq made international news in 1987, when a fisherman landed a great white shark. Locals claimed that it was 7 m (23 ft) long, which would have made it one of the biggest ever discovered. Unfortunately, after scientists did tests with photographs, the shark's size was revealed to be around 5–5.5 m (17–18 ft) in length – big, certainly, but no larger than many other great whites discovered in the Mediterranean.

7 Marsaxlokk

This is Malta's most authentic and delightful fishing port. The harbour is filled with bobbing, brightly coloured *luzzus*. Cobalt-blue fishing nets are spread out along the quays, and countless fish restaurants surround the bay *(see pp26–7)*.

8 Delimara Peninsula

MAP F6

This finger of land is the site of a huge and unsightly power station. Yet, remarkably, the Delimara Peninsula is one of the prettiest corners in all Malta. Neat vegetable and flower plots are interspersed with stretches of wilder country with undulating fields, and there are some wonderful swimming holes. The best of them is the pretty little cove of St Peter's Pool, where the limestone cliffs have been eroded into ice-cream curves and the water is incredibly blue.

Bathers on the rocks at St Peter's Pool

9 Marsaskala
MAP F5

An overgrown fishing village that still retains its fishing fleet, Marsaskala has become one of the biggest resorts at the south of the island. Despite its size, it has a sleepy charm, and even in July and August, when the town is crammed to the gills, it's still quieter and less frenzied than the northern resorts. Families stroll along the harbourfront during the evening *passeggiata*, watching the fishermen mending their nets, before heading to one of the town's popular seafood restaurants. For great swimming and snorkelling, walk around the headland to nearby St Thomas's Bay, which is extremely popular with the Maltese.

Boats in the harbour at Marsaskala

10 St John the Evangelist Chapel, Ħal Millieri, Żurrieq
MAP D6 ▪ 2122 5952 ▪ Visits by appointment ▪ www.dinlarthelwa.org

This tiny, stone-built chapel near the tranquil little town of Żurrieq was built on the remnants of an older chapel and was consecrated in 1480. It was the parish church of Casal Millieri, an ancient village that has long since disappeared, leaving just the chapel in its grove of lofty pines. Inside, the arched vault is divided into five bays, each beautifully decorated with frescoes depicting various saints, including St George enthusiastically finishing off the dragon. The frescoes were buried under layers of whitewash for many years and their bottom sections are irredeemably damaged.

A TOUR AROUND SOUTHERN MALTA

▶ MORNING

Arrive at **Wied Iż-Żurrieq** early to avoid the long queues for the **Blue Grotto**. It's at its best in the bright morning sunshine when the water is a vivid electric blue. After the boat trip into the cave, head to **Marsaxlokk**, which is a tricky drive because there are few signs (take the **Kirkop–Gudja–Ghaxaq** route to avoid getting lost in the Ħal Far industrial estate). Once in this charming fishing port, go for a leisurely stroll around the harbour and admire the multicoloured *luzzus* bobbing up and down in the bay, before enjoying an alfresco lunch. For some of the freshest seafood and lovely harbour views, get a table on the water's edge at one of the many restaurants that are spread out along the port.

AFTERNOON

After lunch, drive (or take a stroll) out to **St Peter's Pool** on the Delimara Peninsula. Fishermen will also ferry passengers from Marsaxlokk harbour to the little cove. Spend a couple of hours sunbathing and swimming in the pool's transparent waters. Then hop into the car for the short drive to the traditional fishing village of **Marsaskala**, where you should just be in time to join the local families in their evening *passeggiata* around the harbour. Stop for a drink in one of the seafront cafés here before pondering where to have dinner. If you're in need of a bite to eat, head to **Carmen's Bar** *(see p99)*, which offers fabulous views across the water.

See map on pp94–5

Churches and Chapels

① Chapel of Our Lady of Providence, near Siġġiewi

MAP C5 ■ 2 km (1 mile) from Siġġiewi on Għar Lapsi road

This dainty and colourful octagonal chapel is usually closed, but opens for the *festa* (feast) of Our Lady of Providence in September.

② St Nicholas, Siġġiewi

MAP C5 ■ Pjazza San Nicolas ■ 2146 0827 ■ *Festa* last Sun in Jun

Designed by the prestigious Baroque architect Lorenzo Gafa, this huge, stately church dominates Pjazza San Nicholas, Siġġiewi's central square.

③ Chapel of Our Lady of Graces, Żabbar

MAP E5 ■ Triq Is-Santwarju ■ 2182 4383 ■ *Festa* first Sun after 8 Sep

The pink, frilly domes of this Baroque church, also called the Żabbar Sanctuary, dominate the town's traffic-blighted old centre. A museum contains sailors' ex-votos.

④ Our Lady of the Annunciation, Tarxien

MAP E5 ■ Triq Il-Kbira ■ 2182 8153 ■ *Festa* fifth Sun after Easter

This elegant 17th-century parish church sits serenely at the centre of a confusing maze of narrow streets.

⑤ St Catherine's, Żejtun

MAP E5 ■ Main square ■ 2169 4563 ■ *Festa* Jun (date varies)

The grandiose 17th-century parish church dominates this languid village. Designed by Lorenzo Gafa, it overlooks the square.

⑥ Old St Gregory's, Żejtun

MAP E5 ■ Triq San Girgor ■ 2167 7187 ■ Open for Mass weekends ■ *Festa* first Wed after Easter

Built in 1436, this simple white-washed structure, topped with a shallow dome and bell tower, is one of the oldest surviving churches in Malta.

⑦ Bir Miftuħ Chapel, Gudja

MAP E5 ■ Gudja ■ 2122 0358 ■ *Festa* 15 Aug

This graceful 15th-century church, dedicated to St Mary of the Open Well, now stands too close for comfort to the runways of Malta's international airport. Inside are the faded remnants of 17th-century murals and an altar painting dating from the 16th century depicting God surrounded by angels.

Exterior of St Mary in Qrendi

⑧ St Mary, Qrendi

MAP D6 ■ Triq Il-Knisja ■ 2164 9395 ■ *Festa* 15 Aug

Lorenzo Gafa transformed an older building into this handsome Baroque parish church in the pretty village of Qrendi. The rivalry between it and that of neighbouring Mqabba is legendary.

⑨ St George's Chapel, Birżebbuġa

MAP E6 ■ St George's Bay, Borġ In-Nadur ■ Mass in English 9:30am Sun

Built by the Knights in 1683, this is the only fortified church on the coast.

⑩ Christ the King, Paola

MAP E5 ■ Pjazza de Paule ■ 2169 5022

Giuseppe D'Amato's modern church overlooks Paola's dreary suburban sprawl. D'Amato was also architect of the huge church in Xewkija, on the island of Gozo *(see p44).*

Restaurants and Cafés

PRICE CATEGORIES
For a three-course meal for one with half a bottle of wine (or equivalent meal), taxes and extra charges.

€ under €30   €€ €30–€50   €€€ over €50

1 Zonqor Point, Marsaskala

MAP F5 ■ Triq Għar ix-Xama ■ 7970 4560 ■ Closed Mon & Tue L (Wed D in winter) ■ €

Specializing in Mediterranean cuisine, this friendly restaurant has been serving excellent fish for over 25 years.

2 Ir-Rizzu, Marsaxlokk

MAP F5 ■ 52 Xatt is-Sajjieda ■ 2165 1569 ■ Closed Sun D ■ €

Fresh fish is the speciality at this great family-run restaurant overlooking the magnificent harbour. Book for Sunday lunch after the quayside fish market.

3 Blue Creek Bar & Restaurant, Għar Lapsi

MAP C6 ■ Għar Lapsi ■ 2146 2800 ■ Closed Mon ■ €€

This smart, family-friendly spot looks out over the sea and the lido formed by a rocky inlet. For lunch, it also has an inexpensive snack menu.

4 La Favorita, Marsaskala

MAP F5 ■ Triq Il-Gardiel ■ 2163 4113 ■ Closed Mon ■ €

This friendly restaurant comes highly recommended by locals for its seafood specialities and relaxed atmosphere. It's located on the edge of town, near St Thomas's Bay. It's best to book at weekends.

5 La Reggia, Marsaxlokk

MAP E5 ■ 110 Xatt is-Sajjieda ■ 9985 5305 ■ Closed Mon, Sun D ■ €€

With a picturesque harbourside setting, this place is a great choice after wandering around Marsaxlokk's Sunday morning fish market. Seafood dishes are the speciality, alongside modern Mediterranean cuisine.

6 Bongo Nyah, Marsaskala

MAP F5 ■ 3 Triq Il-Gardiel ■ 9985 5057 ■ Closed Mon ■ €

This spot has an easy-going, coffeehouse vibe and serves comfort food, salads and healthy smoothies.

7 Tal-Familja, Marsaskala

MAP F5 ■ Triq Il-Gardiel ■ 2163 2161 ■ Closed Mon ■ €€

This spacious restaurant with rustic decor is great for local fish and Maltese cuisine. Daily specials are chalked up on a blackboard.

8 Nargile Lounge, Marsaskala

MAP F5 ■ Triq Il-Gardiel ■ 2163 6734 ■ Closed Tue ■ €

An authentic Arab-style *shisha* lounge; enjoy Indian, Arabic and Mediterranean cuisine, speciality teas and a fruity hookah pipe.

9 Opera Caffe Lounge, Marsaxlokk

MAP F5 ■ 74 Xatt is-Sajjieda ■ 7930 4873 ■ €

Sit out on the harbourside watching the fishing boats while tucking into a fish dinner – your catch will have came off one of those boats that morning. It's also a great place for lunch, coffee or a cocktail.

Elegantly set table with local seafood

10 Carmen's Bar, Għar Lapsi

MAP C6 ■ Limits of Siġġiewi ■ 2146 7305 ■ €

Tuck into some fresh fish or enjoy a drink at this friendly restaurant with a casual vibe and lovely views.

See map on pp94–5 ←

TOP 10 Gozo and Comino

Gozo is smaller, greener and quieter than its big sister, Malta. At its heart is Victoria (sometimes called Rabat), the miniature capital of this island crowned by its Citadel. Nearby, the Ġgantija Temples are among the oldest stone buildings in the world. The Gozitan coastline is breathtaking, particularly at Dwejra, and the whole island is a walker's paradise. There are sandy beaches and countless coves and bays offering good spots for a dip. Smaller still, Comino is poised between Malta and Gozo; wild and largely empty, it has just one hotel. Droves of tourists descend daily to see the lovely Blue Lagoon, but the island always returns to its habitual slumber.

The Citadel at Victoria, a walled metropolis watching over the city below

GOZO AND COMINO

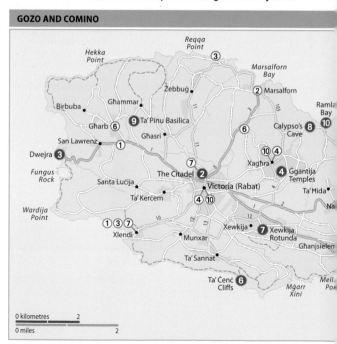

A boat tour visiting the clear azure waters of the Blue Lagoon

1 Blue Lagoon, Comino
The main draw on Comino is the magical Blue Lagoon, the focus of many daily boat cruises. Those staying on the island can enjoy it without the hordes of day-trippers *(see p35)*.

2 The Citadel, Victoria
At the physical and spiritual heart of Gozo, this tiny walled city sits high on a rocky bluff, with commanding views of virtually the whole island. A citadel has existed here since Roman times, but the current structure was built in the 17th century. Gozitans still refer to their capital as Rabat, even though it was officially renamed Victoria to celebrate the British Queen's Diamond Jubilee in 1897 *(see pp30–31)*.

3 Dwejra
The sheer cliffs, curving bays, gigantic caves and entrancing rock formations on this stretch of coastline combine to make it Gozo's best-loved photo opportunity. Tourists flock to Dwejra Point but it is possible to strike out along the cliff paths to enjoy the view in relative peace *(see pp32–3)*.

4 Ġgantija Temples, Xagħra
MAP E1 ■ Triq Parisot ■ 2155 3194 ■ Open daily 9am–4:30pm ■ Adm ■ www.heritagemalta.org
The huge, pale stones of Ġgantija have stood for more than five and a half millennia – over a thousand years longer than the Great Pyramids of Egypt. The sturdy walls reach up to 7 m (23 ft) in height *(see p42)*.

Blas
ay

Daħlet
Qorrot
Bay

Bin Ġemma

Gozo

15

Qala ● 5
8
15

Qasam

ġarr

9 5 Santa Marija
Bay
1 *Comino*
Blue
Lagoon 9

Neolithic temple complex at Ġgantija

5 Santa Marija Bay, Comino
MAP A1

There are two attractive bays, both with sought-after strips of sand, on the island of Comino, but this one is public while the other is private. Out of season you may well find you have it all to yourself *(see p34)*.

Flora growing on a cliff at Ta' Ċenċ

6 Ta' Ċenċ Cliffs
MAP E2

This stretch of wild cliffs, which plunge sheerly into the sea below, is one of the most beautiful sights in Gozo. Go at dusk, when the cliffs are flushed pink by the setting sun. For centuries, bird-trappers swung down these cliffs in rough slings on ropes. Hunting and trapping are now banned, but were once prevalent and the local bird population has suffered

as a result. Nonetheless, numerous bird species continue to make the Ta' Ċenċ cliffs their home *(see p48)*.

7 Xewkija Rotunda
MAP E2 ■ St John the Baptist Square ■ 2155 6793 ■ Open daily for Mass

Just as the Mosta Dome dominates much of the island of Malta, so the Xewkija Rotunda is visible from almost everywhere in Gozo. Villagers claim it is Europe's third-largest dome, although the people of Mosta claim theirs is bigger. Architect Giuseppe D'Amato was inspired by the Basilica of Santa Maria Della Salute in Venice. His church is made of local limestone. It was begun in 1951 and took over 20 years to build *(see p44)*.

8 Calypso's Cave, Ramla Bay
MAP E1 ■ Follow signs from Xagħra ■ Open 9am–dusk

In this cave, carved out of the rock high above Ramla Bay, the love-sick nymph Calypso is said to have seduced Odysseus in Homer's epic *The Odyssey*. Get there by scrambling up the short but steep path that leads from the beachfront or via the road (ask at the café for directions). Although the cave has collapsed and is closed, you can stroll to the view-point to enjoy the stunning scenery. Gazing out at the cobalt sea, it's easy to imagine Odysseus reluctant to leave the island and its resident nymph. You can also view the ruins of an 18th-century fortification built by the Knights of Malta for defence against invaders.

Ochre sands and crystal-clear waters at Ramla Bay

THE XAGĦRA CIRCLE

An underground burial chamber similar to the famous Ħal Saflieni Hypogeum *(see pp28–9)* is being excavated near the Ġgantija Temples. The early excavation notes for the Hypogeum were lost, so the exploration of the Xagħra Circle has enormous importance for archaeologists seeking to understand the world of the Maltese temple-builders. This site was neither as large nor as lavishly decorated as Ħal Saflieni, but ongoing excavations have advanced understanding of pre-historic burial rites to a huge degree.

Ta' Pinu Basilica

9 Ta' Pinu Basilica, Għarb
MAP D1 ■ Triq Ta' Pinu ■ 2155
6045 ■ Open 7am–6:30pm Mon–Sat,
8:15am–5pm Sun

The Ta' Pinu Basilica is Gozo's most
important place of pilgrimage. Our
Lady of Ta' Pinu is credited with
miraculous healing powers, and
numerous ex-votos attest to prayers
being answered. The huge modern
church (which was completed in
1931) retains a section of the original
19th-century chapel where, in 1883,
a local woman is reputed to have
heard the voice of Our Lady (see p45).
There is a museum on site.

10 Ramla Bay
MAP E1

Ramla Bay has Gozo's best beach,
backed by gentle hills with tumbling
terraces. Out of season, it feels like a
corner of paradise, but at the height
of the summer it can get unbearably
crowded. Nearby are the ruins of a
Roman villa built on this idyllic spot
almost 2,000 years ago.

A TOUR AROUND GOZO

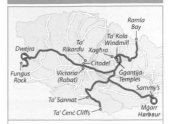

▶ MORNING

Set off early, so that you can
arrive at the cliffs of **Dwejra** (see
pp32–3) in time to enjoy them
without the crowds. Then take
a boat ride from the Inland Sea
through to Dwejra Point. Take
some time to stroll along the cliff
paths and enjoy spectacular
views of **Fungus Rock** and the
rugged coastline. Drive to **Victoria**
to explore the lofty walled **Citadel**
(see pp30–31). Don't miss the
ornate Baroque cathedral. You
can have a simple but delicious
lunch of fresh bread and local
cheese at **Ta' Rikardu** (see p105).

AFTERNOON

After lunch, drive to nearby **Xagħra**
to explore the ancient **Ġgantija
Temples** (see p101), in a beautiful
setting overlooking a wide, green
plain. The same ticket also gains
admission to the **Ta' Kola Windmill**
(see p104) on the outskirts of the
village. Head next to the village
square, where one of the little
café-bars should be open for a
drink. If you have enough time,
you could drive on for another
10 minutes to **Ramla Bay**,
Gozo's best beach, for a
refreshing dip. Then return to the
other side of the island and make
for **Ta' Sannat**, following the signs
for **Ta' Ċenċ**. Spend an enjoyable
hour strolling around these
magnificent cliffs as dusk falls.
Afterwards, dine on fresh fish at
Sammy's (see p105), on the waterfront in **Mġarr Harbour** (see p104),
finishing the day with a drink
at the nearby Gleneagles Bar
(10 Triq Il-Vittorja), which has
a lovely terrace overlooking
the port.

See map on pp100–101 ←

The Best of the Rest

1 Ta' Dbieġi Crafts Village, Għarb

MAP D1 ▪ Triq Franġisk Portelli ▪ Open 9:30am–5pm Mon–Sat

Gozo's craft village is convenient for souvenir shopping. There are demonstrations of traditional crafts, and it's a good place to pick up Gozitan woollen jumpers and rugs.

2 Marsalforn

MAP E1

This pretty fishing village is Gozo's main resort, with a small sandy beach and seafront restaurants. There is a bit of ill-considered modern development but it is still small-scale.

3 Salt Pans, Reqqa Point

MAP D1 ▪ Between Xwieni Bay and Reqqa Point

Hundreds of salt pans indent the soft limestone near Marsalforn, forming a surreal landscape of strange, natural beauty *(see p48)*.

4 Ta' Kola Windmill, Xagħra

MAP E1 ▪ Triq Maija Bambina ▪ 2156 1071 ▪ Open 9am–4:30pm daily ▪ Adm ▪ www.heritagemalta.org

Built in 1725, this is the only survivor of 12 windmills built by the Knights. All kinds of items related to traditional Maltese crafts are gathered here in an interesting little museum.

5 Mġarr Harbour, Mġarr

MAP F2

Guarded by a fortress and hemmed in by cliffs, the focus of Mġarr is still the salty old port, full of colourful *luzzus* and vivid blue fishing nets.

Boats in Mġarr Harbour

6 Folklore Museum, Għarb

MAP D1 ▪ Triq Frenċ ta' l-Għarb ▪ 2156 1929 ▪ Open 9am–4pm Mon–Sat, 9am–1pm Sun ▪ Adm

In one of Gozo's prettiest villages, this engaging little museum has tools, costumes, paintings and curiosities typical of rural Gozitan life.

Exhibit at the Folklore Museum

7 Xlendi Bay

MAP D2

A gentle curve with lots of flat rocks from which to swim and snorkel, Xlendi Bay has a quiet, relaxed vibe and a handful of excellent restaurants.

8 San Blas Bay

MAP F1

This beautiful little bay, with its strip of ochre sand, is hard to reach (you'll need to scramble down a steep footpath), but it's well worth it *(see p48)*.

9 Comino Tower (St Mary's Tower), Comino

MAP A1

It wasn't until 1618 that Comino got fortifications to protect it from pirates. This restored tower still guards the island's southwestern approaches.

10 St George's Basilica, Victoria

MAP D2 ▪ Pjazza San Ġorġ ▪ 2155 6377 ▪ Open for Mass daily

Known as the "Golden Church" because of its dazzling, gilded interior, this sumptuous Baroque edifice was designed by Vittorio Cassar and completed in 1673.

Restaurants and Cafés

1 Ic-Cima, Xlendi
MAP D2 ■ San Xmun ■ 2155
8407 ■ Closed Tue ■ €€

With a terrace looking out over the
bay, this is the perfect place for a
sundowner followed by a delicious
meal of Maltese and Italian food
beautifully presented.

2 Il-Kcina Tal-Barrakka (Sammy's), Mġarr Harbour
MAP F2 ■ 28 Triq de Vilhena ■ 9921
3801 ■ Closed Thu–Tue L, Sun D ■ €€

This harbourside eatery is one of the
best places to try fresh fish. It's run by
the same owners as the Gleneagles
Bar nearby. Book well in advance.

3 Ta' Karolina, Xlendi
MAP D2 ■ Triq L-Ghar ta
Karolina ■ 2155 9675 ■ €€

Right on the water's edge of Xlendi
Bay, this family-run restaurant
serves excellent Mediterranean food
from perfectly fresh fish and meat
mains to pizzas and ice cream.

4 Patrick's, Victoria
MAP D2 ■ Triq Europe ■ 2156
6667 ■ Closed Mon–Sat L, Sun D
(Mon in winter) ■ €€–€€€

An elegant restaurant decorated
with contemporary art, this place
is popular with a well-heeled
local crowd. Go for the six-course
"tasting menu".

5 Zeppi's Pub, Qala
MAP F2 ■ St Joseph Square
■ 9909 8167 ■ Closed Mon L ■ €

This attractive village pub offers a
great range of imaginative lunchtime
snacks, including salads, omelettes
and *croques monsieurs*. There is
music and dancing at night.

6 Ta' Frenc, Xagħra
MAP E1 ■ Triq Ghajn Damma
■ 2155 3888 ■ Closed Tue ■ €€€

This exceptional restaurant, serving
excellent Maltese and Mediterranean
dishes in a stylishly restored
farmhouse, is often considered the
best in all Malta.

7 Ta' Rikardu, Victoria
MAP D2 ■ 4 Triq Il-Fosos ■ 2155
5953 ■ Closed Tue ■ €

Conveniently located right next to
the cathedral in the Citadel, this
rustic little spot serves delicious
local bread, cheese and wine.

Busy with customers, Ta' Rikardu

8 Il-Wileg Qala
MAP F2 ■ 54 Triq Il-Mithna
■ 9988 5482 ■ Mon–Sat L, Sun D ■ €

Flavoursome traditional cuisine and
perfectly cooked fresh fish are served
in a historic Gozitan village guesthouse or in the pretty little courtyard.

9 Blue Lagoon, Comino
MAP F2 ■ San Niklaw Bay
■ 2152 9821 ■ Open Apr–Oct ■ www.
cominohotel.com ■ €

Located in the Comino Hotel *(see
p115)*, this is the only restaurant on
the island; it has a reliable buffet.

10 Dvenue, Xagħra
MAP E1 ■ 32 Victory Square
■ 2156 6542 ■ €€

Gozitan flavours stand out on the
menu here, with homemade pasta
and traditional specialities, such as
rabbit and lamb featuring. There are
options for vegetarians and vegans.

See map on pp100–101 ←

Streetsmart

A typical narrow cobbled street in Valletta

Getting To and Around Malta and Gozo

Arriving by Air

Numerous airlines fly into **Malta International Airport** in Luqa, which is about 8 km (5 miles) from Valletta. The national airline, **Air Malta**, connects with over 35 destinations across Europe, the Middle East and North Africa. Other large carriers, including **British Airways**, **Alitalia**, **Lufthansa** and **Emirates**, also fly to Malta, as do budget airlines **Ryanair** and **easyJet**.

Arriving by Boat

The sea is a great way to arrive in Malta, whether by ferry, cruise liner or yacht. There are beautiful views as you approach the islands, especially when entering the iconic Grand Harbour.

A regular ferry runs from southwestern Sicily right to the lovely Valletta waterfront in the Grand Harbour. It takes around 90 minutes by fast catamaran, which is run by **Virtu Ferries**. Valletta is a stopover on many Mediterranean cruises, which also moor at the modern terminal building on the Grand Harbour. There is a lift rising swiftly from the waterfront up to the Upper Barrakka Gardens providing easy access to Valletta.

An increasing number of private yacht marinas make it easy for those with their own boat to spend time in Malta. The biggest marinas are in Marsamxett Harbour,

between Valletta and Sliema, while there is also a marina on the Vittoriosa Waterfront at Birgu and there are moorings for smaller boats at Mġarr Harbour, Gozo.

Contact the **Maritime Authority**, **Customs Office** and **Royal Malta Yacht Club** for more information.

Getting Around by Bus

Operated by **Malta Public Transport**, Malta has a large, cheap and effective network of bus routes that will take you almost anywhere on the main island. Gozo also has an extensive service run by the same company, but buses are less frequent.

Malta was once known for its much-photographed old British buses. These have now been replaced with modern vehicles that have air-conditioning and are less polluting.

The main terminus on Malta is the **City Gate Bus Station**, located just outside the walls of Valletta, where most buses begin. There are a number of express routes to and from the airport from different locations. The **Victoria Bus Station** is the main terminus on Gozo.

There are various hop-on, hop-off sightseeing buses that run around Malta and Gozo taking in all the major sights. These include **Malta Sightseeing**, which also runs a shuttle that picks up and drops off at hotels, and a "Malta by Night" tour.

Getting Around by Boat

The Gozo ferry (run by the **Gozo Channel Company**) carries people and vehicles between Ċirkewwa (Malta) and Mġarr Harbour (Gozo). It takes half an hour, is inexpensive and runs day and night. There are also some small ferries to Comino from Ċirkewwa and Mġarr.

Passenger ferries run across the two harbours flanking Valletta, to Sliema on one side and to the Three Cities on the other. The ferry is the quickest way of making these journeys.

One of the best ways to see the Maltese islands is by boat. The ferries offer a taste of this, but there are also plenty of boat tours and day trips taking in views of the coast. Companies offering trips include **Sea Adventure Excursions**, **Hornblower Cruises** and **Captain Morgan Cruises**. Most of these start in Sliema and Mġarr (Gozo), although a few run from Mellieha.

Getting Around by Car

A car is a great aid to getting off the beaten track. Malta drives on the left (like the UK) and has similar rules of the road; however, they are not always adhered to. Maltese drivers are not keen on slowing down (especially at roundabouts) and can be unpredictable.

Traffic is quite heavy in parts of the main island. It is less so on Gozo, where everything moves more slowly. Renting a car is easy. Most major firms – including **Avis**, **Europcar** and **Hertz** – have offices at the airport and there are also local companies around the islands

Getting Around by Taxi

The official **Malta Taxis** are white and have fixed fares from the airport to key destinations on the main island. Do confirm the price with your driver before setting off. For other journeys, private taxis are as good and there are plenty of licensed firms

providing cars with drivers for short trips or whole days. Hotels usually have a relationship with a firm that they can recommend.

Much of Valletta is pedestrianized so taxis cannot always drop you right at your destination. If you need help with mobility within the city, **Smart Cabs**, little white golf buggies, are allowed throughout the city. They gather outside St John's Co-Cathedral or can be called in advance. They run until 7pm in winter or 8pm in summer.

Getting Around on Foot

The best way to get around Malta's cities is on foot. Much of Valletta

and the Three Cities is pedestrianized and most towns are small enough to explore on foot. There are some good walking guides available; check them out at Agenda Bookshop.

Getting Around by Bicycle

Given the unpredictability of drivers, cycling on Malta is not the safest way to travel, but visitors do tour by bike and there are quieter routes, particularly on Gozo. In rural areas beware of potholes. If you want to cycle, there is a helpful book available, *Cycling Malta & Gozo* by Joseph Montebello. A good cycle hire company is **EcoBikesMalta**.

DIRECTORY

ARRIVING BY AIR

Air Malta
w airmalta.com

Alitalia
w alitalia.com

British Airways
w britishairways.com

easyJet
w easyjet.com

Emirates
w emirates.com

Lufthansa
w lufthansa.com

Malta International Airport
MAP E5–D5 ▪ Luqa
w maltairport.com

Ryanair
w ryanair.com

ARRIVING BY BOAT

Customs Office
w customs.gov.mt

Maritime Authority
w transport.gov.mt/ports-marinas

Royal Malta Yacht Club
w rmyc.org

Virtu Ferries
w virtuferries.com

GETTING AROUND BY BUS

City Gate Bus Station
MAP H3 ▪ Vjal Nelson, Valletta

Malta Public Transport
w publictransport.com.mt

Malta Sightseeing
w hellomaltatours.com

Victoria Bus Station
MAP D2 ▪ Triq Giorgio Borġ Olivier

GETTING AROUND BY BOAT

Captain Morgan Cruises
w captainmorgan.com.mt

Gozo Channel Company
w gozochannel.com

Hornblower Cruises
w hornblowerboat.com

Sea Adventure Excursions
w seaadventure excursions.com

GETTING AROUND BY CAR

Avis
w avis.com.mt

Europcar
w europcar.com.mt

Hertz
w hertz.com.mt

GETTING AROUND BY TAXI

Malta Taxis
w www.maltairport.com/passenger/getting-here/taxi-service

Smart Cabs
c 7741 4177

GETTING AROUND BY BICYCLE

EcoBikesMalta
w ecobikesmalta.com

Practical Information

Passports and Visas

Visitors from outside the European Economic Area (EEA), European Union (EU) and Switzerland need a valid passport to travel to Malta, as do UK visitors; most other EU nationals require only a valid identity card. Certain nationalities can stay for up to 90 days without a visa, while some will need a visa for any length of visit; for longer stays, a Schengen visa is needed and must be obtained in advance from the nearest Maltese embassy. Check the government's Identity Malta website (www.identitymalta.com) for further details.

The **Australian High Commission** and the **British High Commission** are located in Ta' Xbiex, and the **Maltese Foreign Affairs** website has a directory of other offices.

Customs and Immigration

There are no restrictions on what EU citizens can bring in and out of Malta so long as it is a reasonable quantity for personal use. Those from outside the EU may bring up to 200 cigarettes, a litre of spirits and 1 kg of tobacco.

Travel Safety Advice

Visitors can obtain the most up-to-date travel safety information from the **UK Foreign and Commonwealth Office**, the **US Department of State** and the **Australian Department of Foreign Affairs and Trade**.

Travel Insurance

It is advisable to take out an insurance policy that covers cancellation or curtailment of your trip, theft or loss of money and baggage, and health care.

Personal Safety

Although Malta has quite a low crime rate, adhere to the same precautions you would take elsewhere in Europe.

Call the **emergency number** for the police, fire brigade or ambulance. To report a traffic accident that doesn't need emergency services, call the local **traffic wardens**. These green-uniformed wardens are responsible for road safety.

To report a crime, contact the local police. Each town or village has a police station, spotted by the blue lantern outside. The Malta Police Force wear blue uniforms. The **police headquarters** are located in Floriana (Malta) and Victoria (or Rabat, Gozo).

Beach Safety

Some beaches have flags communicating where and when it is safe to swim. They should always be observed. During, and also after, bad weather there can be dangerous currents. Jellyfish also gather occasionally. The main jellyfish in Malta are not dangerous but their sting does hurt – if flags or locals tell you there are jellyfish, it is best to go to another beach.

Illegal Hunting

Hunting birds was once a relatively popular activity on Malta and the island's bird population suffered as a result. It is now illegal to hunt all birds with the exception of the common quail and there are strict rules in place. However, the hunting ban is sometimes violated and gunshots can occasionally be heard in rural areas. Tourists are not generally at any risk, but it may be sensible to make yourself visible if there is shooting nearby. Contact the conservation group **BirdLife Malta** for information.

Health

Malta has no vaccination requirements and has a good and inexpensive health-care service.

The most common health problems for visitors arise from too much sun: drink plenty of water and use sunscreen or cover up as necessary. Sunglasses are essential, not only on the beach but around the limestone buildings that strongly reflect the sun.

Tap water in Malta is safe to drink but most locals drink bottled water, which is readily available, and visitors are advised to do so too.

There are state-funded clinics (listed on the **Government Health** website), which are free with the European Health Insurance Card (EHIC) and private local doctors (not covered by the EHIC). Private GPs are often based in pharmacies and are not as expensive as in many other countries. Most hotels also have a doctor they can call out (usually private so not covered by the EHIC). The state clinics can also deal with minor accidents usually without a long wait.

Pharmacies, which are identified by a large green cross, are common throughout the country and a Sunday roster is listed on the Government Health website.

The main hospital on Malta is the **Mater Dei Hospital** in Msida, while **Gozo General Hospital** is located in the capital of Gozo, Victoria (Rabat).

Currency and Banking

Malta's currency is the euro. There are banks in all the larger towns and ATMs in some smaller places. Banks are usually open 8:30am–1:30pm Monday–Thursday, 8:30am–3:30pm Friday and 8:30am–12:30pm Saturday. Some banks in larger towns and resorts may open one or two afternoons a week, but those in smaller towns often close on Saturday mornings in summer.

Most restaurants and hotels will accept credit cards although a few of the cheaper guesthouses and small beachside cafés may not. Mastercard and Visa are the most widely accepted, Diners Club and American Express less so.

Communications

The telephone dialling code to Malta is +356 and to make an international call from Malta it is 00. Mobile phones are common and if you are visiting from the EU using your mobile phone here is easy

and inexpensive. Although British-style red phone boxes can still be found they are little used other than for tourist photos. Most do still function but require a phone card; this is called a Telecard and can usually be purchased from newsagents.

Wi-Fi is commonly available. Most hotels and many restaurants offer free Wi-Fi, and there are hotspots outside too, including in Valletta's main square.

The **Maltese Postal Service** is very reliable. Post offices are found in larger towns and usually open 7:30am–12:45pm Monday–Saturday. Main branches, such as those in Valletta on Malta and Victoria (Rabat) on Gozo, stay open until 4:30pm and are also open on Saturday mornings. Post boxes are bright red, an appealing British tradition that has been retained.

DIRECTORY

PASSPORTS AND VISAS

Maltese Foreign Affairs
w foreignaffairs.gov.mt

Australian High Commission
MAP E4
■ Ta' Xbiex Terrace, Ta' Xbiex
[2133 8201
w malta.highcommission.gov.au

British High Commission
MAP E4
■ Whitehall Mansions, Ta'Xbiex Seafront, XBX
[2323 0000
w gov.uk/world/organisations/british-high-commission-malta

TRAVEL SAFETY ADVICE

Australian Department of Foreign Affairs and Trade
w dfat.gov.au
w smartraveller.gov.au

UK Foreign and Commonwealth Office
w gov.uk/foreign-travel-advice

US Department of State
w travel.state.gov

PERSONAL SAFETY

Emergency Number
[112

Police Headquarters
Floriana: MAP E4;
Pjazza San Kalcidonju ;
2294 0019 Victoria (Rabat): MAP D2; Triq Ir-Repubblika; 2156 2040

Traffic Wardens
[2132 0202

ILLEGAL HUNTING

BirdLife Malta
w birdlifemalta.com

HEALTH

Government Health
w health.gov.mt

Gozo General Hospital
MAP D2 ■ Victoria
[2156 1482
w health.gov.mt/en/ggh

Mater Dei Hospital
MAP D4 ■ Triq Dun Karm, Msida
[2545 4182
w health.gov.mt/en/MDH

COMMUNICATIONS

Maltese Postal Service
w maltapost.com

Media

Malta's leading newspaper is the *Times of Malta*, which famously continued to publish every day of World War II. It generally backs the Nationalist Party (conservatives). *The Independent* has less comprehensive coverage, a lower circulation and less clear political links. *Malta Today* is published twice weekly and is unaffiliated. All three are in the English language. *In-Nazzjon* and *L-Orizzont* are the main Maltese-language papers. British and other European publications are readily available in larger towns.

There are three main TV stations in Malta. One is publicly owned, another is owned by the Labour Party and the third by the Nationalist Party. Cable and satellite are hugely popular and most hotels have satellite television.

There are also many radio stations, mostly playing popular, easy listening music. Some are in English, including **Magic Malta** and **Kiss FM**.

Shopping

Shops are generally open 9am–noon and 4–7pm on weekdays. Some close one afternoon a week, many are shut Saturday afternoons and most close all day on Sunday. Department stores tend not to close in the middle of the day and some in larger shopping centres stay open later in the evening too. In tourist areas, particularly in summer, many shops are open all day, including at the weekend.

Malta is known for its silver filigree, colourful Mdina glass and lace. Most souvenir lace is machine made; handmade lace is expensive because it takes a staggeringly long time to make. Handicrafts can be bought in specialist shops in Valletta, Victoria and elsewhere or in the "craft villages" at Ta' Qali (see p92) on Malta and Ta' Dbieġi on Gozo. Here you can also see demonstrations of silverwork, lace- and glass-making.

Time Difference

Malta is two hours ahead of GMT in the summer and one hour ahead of GMT in the winter. This makes it six hours ahead of New York and nine hours ahead of California.

Electrical Appliances

Most sockets in Malta are the British-style three-square-pin plugs. Some hotels also have European-style plugs. Electricity is at 230–240V, 50Hz.

Weather

Malta has a very typical Mediterranean climate: hot, sunny summers, mild winters, and low rainfall. In spring and autumn the islands can be affected by the *sirocco*, desert winds from Africa. In winter, the bitingly cold *gregale* brings occasional storms. July and August are the hottest months, while September and October are the wettest. Sea water stays warm from early summer well into autumn.

Malta's high season runs from late June to mid-September. There is a lot to be said for avoiding the peak time, however, as September and early October are usually still hot enough for the beach. Spring is fresh and beautiful and both spring and autumn are perfect times for sightseeing.

Travellers with Specific Needs

Malta is getting better at providing for those with specific needs. Quite a few hotels now have accessible rooms. Museums and sights are doing their best, but in 16th-century buildings it can be difficult. Most buses have low doors for easy access and the Gozo ferry is fully accessible to wheelchair users.

The website for the **National Commission Persons with Disability** has contact details and practical information for travellers with special needs. **Wheelchair Friendly Car Hire** specializes in renting out accessible cars in Malta.

Sources of Information

The **Malta Tourism Authority (MTA)** website is useful as a first port of call when planning your trip. There is lots of information about sights, activities, festivals and events as well as an interactive map. For Gozo, there is **Visit Gozo**, the official website of Gozo's ministry for tourism.

The MTA has offices in Australia and in many European countries, including the UK. There are plenty of helpful MTA offices in Malta too, including at the airport, in Valletta, Marsaxlokk and Mdina in Malta and at Victoria (Rabat) in Gozo. The addresses of all these offices are listed on the MTA website.

Language

Maltese and English are the official languages and almost all Maltese speak both. Maltese is closely related to Arabic, but uses a lot of European, especially Italian, vocabulary and the Latin alphabet with a few special marks (see p126). Signs are often bilingual but occasionally in only one of the two languages.

Trips and Tours

There are plenty of short tours offered in Malta, from boat trips to Comino's Blue Lagoon to bus tours of the capital (see p108). Day trips to Gozo are a popular option with those based on the main island, as are trips to Valletta and Mdina in the north.

Walking tours are offered by Colour My Travel (www. colourmytravel.com).

Where to Eat

Malta has a burgeoning culinary scene. A number of ethnicities are represented in the islands' restaurants but the best food is Mediterranean, including Malta's own national dishes and much from across the water in Sicily and mainland Italy.

The Maltese love their food and portions are generous. Service can be slow at times. An acceptable tip is normally 10–15 per cent of the bill.

The Definitive(ly) Good Guide to Restaurants is online and published annually in a pocket-sized book form. This gourmet bible reflects the opinions of restaurant-goers rather than critics. It has categories for all sorts of requirements from type of cuisine to location and family-friendly places. The maps are also useful.

Where To Stay

Malta has plenty of visitor beds, from five-star chain hotels and contemporary boutiques to all-inclusive resorts and self-catering Gozitan farmhouses. B&Bs are becoming popular, particularly in Gozo, as are designer conversions of historic buildings.

Self-catering has spread from the waterside apartments of Sliema, Buġibba and Marsalforn to the 16th-century streets of Valletta where you can now live in your own flat at a reasonable cost. Local companies specializing in this area include **Baron Holiday Homes, Holiday Malta, Mellieħa Holiday Centre, Gozo Prestige Holidays** and **Palazzo Prince D'Orange**.

Prices vary a lot through the year. Summer is most expensive, although in Valletta the high season includes September and much of October. The larger hotels in Malta price their rooms by occupancy, which means that in low season, five-star resort hotels can be a real bargain. It is worth checking directly with the hotel for the best price, though package deals can also offer the best prices to some hotels.

DIRECTORY

MEDIA

The Independent
w independent.com.mt

In-Nazzjon
w netnews.com.mt

Kiss FM
91.3 MHz

L-Orizzont
w inewsmalta.com

Magic Malta
91.7 MHz

Malta Today
w maltatoday.com.mt

Times of Malta
w timesofmalta.com

TRAVELLERS WITH SPECIFIC NEEDS

National Commission Persons with Disability
w crpd.org.mt

Wheelchair Friendly Car Hire
c 9949 3963

SOURCES OF INFORMATION

Malta Tourism Authority (MTA)
w mta.com.mt/mta

Visit Gozo
w visitgozo.com

WHERE TO EAT

The Definite(ly) Good Guide to Restaurants
w restaurantsmalta.com

WHERE TO STAY

Baron Holiday Homes
w baronholidayhomes.com

Gozo Prestige Holidays
w gozoprestigeholidays.com

Holiday Malta
w holiday-malta.com

Mellieħa Holiday Centre
w www.mhc.com.mt

Palazzo Prince D'Orange
w palazzoprincemalta.com

Places to Stay

> **PRICE CATEGORIES**
> For a standard, double room per night (with breakfast if included), taxes and extra charges.
>
> € under €120 €€ €120–€240 €€€ over €240

Luxury Retreats

The Palace Malta, Sliema
MAP Q3 ■ Triq il-Kbira ■ 2133 3444 ■ www.the palacemalta.com ■ €€
In a traditional residential area between Sliema's shops and the seafront, this excellent hotel is equipped with stylish rooms. Amenities include a spa, a fitness room and an indoor and outdoor rooftop swimming pool. Temptasian, the restaurant on the top floor, offers superb views of Valletta.

Ta' Ċenċ, Sannat, Gozo
MAP E2 ■ 2155 6819 ■ Closed early Jan–early Feb ■ www.tacenc.com ■ €€
The romantic, village-style Ta' Ċenċ's low-rise rooms are built with creamy limestone; the circular *trullos* (bungalows with beehive shaped roofs) are most desirable. There's a spa, gardens, pools, a gym and an outdoor restaurant. A shuttle bus serves the beach club during high season.

Hilton Malta, St Julian's
MAP P1 ■ Portomaso ■ 2138 3383 ■ www. malta.hilton.com ■ €€–€€€
Set along the picturesque Portomaso Yacht Marina, the hotel features spacious guest rooms, on-site restaurants and bars. There are indoor and outdoor pools, a spa, a gym, a dance studio, tennis and squash courts.

Kempinski Hotel San Lawrenz, Gozo
MAP D1 ■ Triq Ir-Rokon ■ 2211 0000 ■ www. kempinski.com/gozo ■ €€–€€€
Built of creamy stone and located at the edge of a traditional village, this is a stylish and tranquil retreat. It has pleasant gardens and outdoor and indoor pools, as well as possibly Malta's finest spa, offering Ayurveda, and other health and beauty treatments.

Corinthia Hotel, St George's Bay
MAP N1 ■ St Julian's ■ 2137 4114 ■ www. corinthia.com ■ €€€
Right on the seashore, this resort hotel offers guests a choice of seven outdoor and one indoor pool, as well as private access to the sea. Restaurants include a fine dining place, an American diner, an Asian restaurant and a poolside bar.

The Phoenicia, Valletta
MAP G3 ■ Triq il-Mall, Floriana ■ 2122 5241 ■ www.campbellygray hotels.com ■ €€€
Set in an elegant 16th-century palazzo, the Phoenicia offers comfortable accommodation, chic restaurants, plush bars and an outdoor pool. With commanding views of the Grand Harbour and the city skyline, it is also within a walking distance of Valletta's attractions.

Radisson Blu Resort and Spa, Malta Golden Sands, Golden Bay
MAP A3 ■ 2356 1000 ■ www.radissonblu.com ■ €€€
Huge and glossy, this resort hotel overlooks one of Malta's best beaches and offers every five-star luxury. It has extensive sports facilities, a large spa, and a private sandy beach. It is also very family-friendly and the only hotel on the bay.

Characterful Places to Stay

Hotel Juliani, St Julian's
MAP N1 ■ 25 Triq San Ġorġ ■ 2138 8000 ■ www. hoteljuliani.com ■ €
Malta's first boutique hotel is still the epitome of seaside charm and urban style, which combines antique and contemporary furnishings. Its restaurants and bars are the most fashionable on buzzy Spinola Bay. The tiny rooftop pool and deck offer fabulous views.

Murella Living, Marsalforn, Gozo
MAP E1 ■ Triq il-Forn ■ 2155 0340 ■ www. murellaliving.com ■ €
A short distance from Marsalforn's seafront, this

designer boutique hotel is an excellent value place to stay. Each innovatively decorated room is inspired by a modern take on a classical Gozitan sight or traditional motif. The continental breakfast is very good.

Quaint Hotel, Nadur

MAP E2 ■ Triq ta 'Dicembru 13 ■ 2210 8500 ■ www.quaint hotels.com ■ €
Set in the main village square, this modern boutique hotel offers twelve rooms, including three penthouses, that are uniquely styled and decorated. There are on-site restaurants and a rooftop terrace.

Valletta G-House, Valletta

MAP J2 ■ Triq it-Tramuntana ■ 7765 4321 ■ www.vallettahouse. com ■ €–€€
This unusual, charming and romantic townhouse is set in a beautiful historic building. It is decorated with objets d'art, paintings and antiques, but it has modern amenities so you can make yourself at home in Valletta.

B&B Dar ta' Zeppi, Qala, Gozo

MAP F2 ■ 39 28th April 1688 Street ■ 2155 5051 ■ Closed mid-Dec–mid-Jan ■ www.dartazeppi. com ■ €€
This comfortable B&B offers five en-suite rooms, a garden and pool area. Art historian and cook-extraordinaire, Tanja, prepares dinner or a BBQ while husband Vince prepares drinks. An on-site gallery displays artwork by local artists.

Corinthia Palace Hotel and Spa, Attard

MAP C4 ■ De Paule Avenue ■ 2144 0301 ■ www.corinthia.com/ palace ■ €€
The birthplace of the international Corinthia brand, this five-star hotel offers excellent facilities, such as indoor and outdoor pools, a lovely Mediterranean garden, a spa and four stylish restaurants.

SU29, Valletta

MAP J3 ■ 29 Triq Sant' Orsla ■ 2124 2929 ■ www. su29hotel.com ■ €€
This sleek, modern designer boutique hotel is in a historic Valletta house near the Grand Harbour. Each of the eight rooms is different, ranging from traditional, with a typical enclosed wooden balcony, to the "fitness suite" complete with punch bag.

Ursulino, Valletta

MAP J3 ■ Triq Sant' Orsla ■ 2122 8024 ■ www.ursu linovalletta.com ■ €€
An original Valletta townhouse has been coverted into this modern boutique hotel featuring a roof terrace with views of the Grand Harbour. Each evening on the roof, an aperitif and canapés are included for guests. The excellent breakfast can be taken on the roof too.

Xara Palace, Mdina

MAP C4 ■ Misraħ Il-Kunsill ■ 2145 0560 ■ www.xarapalace.com. mt ■ €€€
This hotel is housed in a magnificent 17th-century palace within the walls of the "Silent City". It is

the perfect spot to soak up Mdina's buzzing atmosphere when the tour groups have left. Its restaurants, particularly de Mondion (see p93), are superb.

Seaside Charmers

Comino Hotel, Comino

MAP F2 ■ San Niklaw Bay ■ 2152 9821 ■ Open May–Oct ■ www.comino hotel.com ■ €
The only accommodation on Comino, this hotel overlooks a bay and private beach – an ideal place to relax once the day-trippers have left. Rooms are simple, but there are good sports facilities. Prices are for half-board.

Maria Giovanna Guesthouse, Gozo

MAP E1 ■ Marsalforn Bay ■ 2155 3630 ■ www. tamariagozo.com ■ €
A delightful budget option, this traditional stone townhouse has been refurbished and each room has en-suite facilities. Restaurants and nightlife are nearby and it's also easy to get away into the country.

St Patrick's Hotel, Xlendi, Gozo

MAP D2 ■ Xatt Ix-Xlendi ■ 2156 2951 ■ www.st patrickshotel.com ■ €
This smart, whitewashed hotel is ideally located right by the sea. Some rooms have terraces overlooking the bay, as well as Jacuzzis. There's a small rooftop pool with a sun deck, perfect for unwinding with a drink. The restaurant serves a buffet English breakfast.

Grand Hotel, Gozo

MAP E2 ▪ 58 Triq Sant' Anton, Mġarr ▪ 2216 1000 ▪ www.grand hotelmalta.com ▪ €–€€

From its commanding position on the hill above Mġarr Harbour, the Grand gives amazing views of the port and its painted fishing boats. Most of the guest rooms have balconies that overlook the port. There is an inviting rooftop pool, a restaurant with a summer terrace, and a spa with sauna and Jacuzzi.

San Andrea, Xlendi, Gozo

MAP D2 ▪ St Xlendi Promenade ▪ 2156 5555 ▪ www.hotelsanandrea. com ▪ €–€€

With a bayside location, this intimate hotel offers 28 pretty rooms. Modern, but traditional in style, with archways and iron grilles, the hotel has a restaurant with great views.

Cavalieri Art Hotel, St Julian's

MAP N1 ▪ Triq Spinola ▪ 2318 0000 ▪ www.cava lierihotel.com.mt ▪ €€

This four-star hotel with spacious rooms is situated at the tip of St Julian's Bay, next to Spinola Bay. Its waterfront location offers great views and close proximity to many restaurants, bars and shops. There are outdoor and indoor pools.

Victoria Hotel, Sliema

MAP Q3 ▪ Triq Ġorġ Borġ Olivier ▪ 2133 4711 ▪ www. victoriahotel.com ▪ €€

The Victoria features an elegant interior that evokes a 19th-century gentlemen's club. It is not far from the seafront, and shares some facilities with the neighbouring five-star hotel, The Palace.

Marina Hotel Corinthia Beach Resort, St Julian's

MAP D3 ▪ St George's Bay ▪ 2370 2000 ▪ www. marinahotel.com.mt ▪ €€– €€€

A bright and airy hotel conveniently in St George's Bay. All rooms have private balconies with panoramic views of the bay. The hotel's pools and beach are shared with the Corinthia Hotel next door.

Family-Friendly Hotels

Ambassador Hotel, St Paul's Bay

MAP B3 ▪ Xemxija ▪ 2157 3870 ▪ www.ambassador malta.com ▪ €

Just across the road from the sea, the Ambassador offers bright, good-value accommodation, a wine bar and restaurant, and a large swimming pool. It's only a short hop on the bus to the nearby sands at Ghadira Bay.

Bayview Hotel & Apartments, Sliema

MAP E4 ▪ 143 Triq Ix-Xatt ▪ 2134 6212 ▪ www.bay viewmalta.com ▪ €

Sitting on the waterfront, this simple property has indoor and outdoor pools, a games room, a gym and a wellness centre for adults. Some rooms offer kitchenettes.

Ramla Bay Resort, Marfa

MAP B2 ▪ Triq Il-Marfa ▪ 2281 2281 ▪ www. ramlabayresort.com ▪ €

Situated on a small bay, this resort is good for families who want a quiet break. Facilities include indoor and outdoor pools, a spa, a small sandy beach and an on-site scuba diving school.

Dolmen Resort Hotel, St Paul's Bay

MAP C3 ▪ Qawra ▪ 2355 2355 ▪ www.dolmen. com.mt ▪ €–€€

Located just across the road from the waterfront, this hotel is named after some fascinating mega-lithic remains in the gardens. There are good-value family rooms and a summer Kids' Club. Parents can relax at the spa and there are four pools set in lush gardens.

be.Hotel, St Julian's

MAP D3 ▪ Bay Street Complex, St George's Bay ▪ 2138 4421 ▪ www.be hotelmalta.com ▪ €€

Ideal for families with teenagers, this is part of a large shopping and entertainment complex, near the buzzy nightlife of Paceville. Family rooms and studio apartments with small kitchenettes are available. There's a rooftop pool and a small spa and beauty centre, and it's just a couple of minutes' walk from a sandy beach.

Cornucopia, Xaghra, Gozo

MAP E1 ▪ 10 Triq Gnien Imrik ▪ 2155 6486 ▪ www. cornucopiahotel.com ▪ €€

A converted farmhouse forms the heart of this complex, which is set around a flower-filled courtyard with a pool; there's also a children's pool. The bungalows across the road are more comfortable for families.

Westin Dragonara Resort, St Julian's

MAP D3 ▪ Triq Dragonara ▪ 2138 1000 ▪ www.west inmalta.com ▪ €€
One of Malta's most lavish resorts, the vast Westin Dragonara has something to entertain everyone, including a private sandy cove, two outdoor and one indoor pool, health and beauty facilities and activities for family entertainment – from sports tournaments to painting lessons. With children in mind, there are colouring books in the restaurants and electrical outlet covers in bedrooms.

Xlendi Resort & Spa, Xlendi, Gozo

MAP D2 ▪ Triq San Xmun ▪ 2755 3719 ▪ €€
The Xlendi Hotel overlooks the spectacular Xlendi Bay. Spa facilities include an indoor pool and hot tub, and a sauna. It also has a pool on the roof, and a restaurant on the roof terrace. All of the bedrooms have free Wi-Fi and air-conditioning.

Db Seabank Resort & Spa, Mellieħa

MAP B2 ▪ Triq Il-Marfa ▪ 2289 1000 ▪ www.db hotelsresorts.com ▪ €€– €€€
Located just across the road from this modern all-inclusive hotel is probably the best sandy beach in Malta, certainly its longest, with bars, cafés and watersports. The hotel itself has several dining options, including a child-friendly jungle-themed restaurant. There are indoor and outdoor pools, a gym, a bowling alley and a spa.

Budget Hotels and Guesthouses

Corner Hostel, Sliema

MAP P2 ▪ 6 Triq Santa Margerita ▪ 2780 2780 ▪ €
Very close to the beach, this is an unusual option for Malta: a hostel offering both en-suite rooms and dormitories, and a 24-hour communal kitchen.

Hostel Jones, Sliema

MAP P2 ▪ Triq Sir Adrian Dingli ▪ 9932 0003 ▪ www.maltahostel.com ▪ €
Set in an ideal location, Hostel Jones is headed by a young team that lends it a fresh vibe. It offers good facilities and only double rooms, which have a distinct appeal and provide value for money.

Lantern Guesthouse, Marsalforn, Gozo

MAP E1 ▪ Triq Qbajjar ▪ 2155 6285 ▪ www.gozo. com/lantern ▪ €
Offering simple en-suite rooms and basic apart-ments, this guesthouse is particularly good value for families or groups. There is a small fee for air-conditioning, but the rooms are equipped with fans. An inexpensive restaurant and pizzeria are located downstairs.

Mariblu Guesthouse, Xewkija, Gozo

MAP E2 ▪ Triq L-Imġarr ▪ 2155 1315 ▪ www.gozo boutiquehotel.accommo dation.com ▪ €
This is a family-run, friendly guesthouse in a sleepy Gozitan village famous for its parish church. The rooms, all with en-suite bathrooms, are above the Mariblu restaurant in the village

centre. Other facilities include two pools and a dive centre.

Point de Vue, Rabat

MAP C4 ▪ 2/7 Is-Saqqajja ▪ 2145 4117 ▪ www.point devue-mdina.com ▪ €
Be sure to book ahead for rooms in this family-run guesthouse, which is just outside the main gate to the "Silent City".

Primera Hotel, Buġibba

MAP C3 ▪ Pioneer Rd ▪ 2157 3880 ▪ www. primerahotel.com ▪ €
The modern hotel has a good central location and reasonable facilities. There are indoor and outdoor pools, a kids' paddling pool, and a rooftop terrace for sun-bathing. Rooms are plain but air-conditioned and they all have satellite TV.

San Antonio Guest-house, Xlendi, Gozo

MAP D2 ▪ Tower Street ▪ 2156 3555/9949 6807 ▪ www.clubgozo.com.mt ▪ €
This simple but charming little guesthouse on the cliffs above Xlendi Bay has a lovely little swim-ming pool and is just a short walk into the village.

Splendid Guesthouse, Mellieħa

MAP B3 ▪ Il-Triq Kappillan Magri ▪ 9919 2149 ▪ www.splendid-guest-house.business.site ▪ €
Bright rooms, with either full en-suite facilities or a shower, a bar and restaurant, Wi-Fi, and a sun terrace make this the best budget deal in Mellieħa. The beach is a bus-ride away, but shops and nightlife are close by.

For a key to hotel price categories see p114

Index

Acknowledgments

Author

Mary-Ann Gallagher is a widely experienced travel writer, now based in Barcelona. She has written and contributed to several Dorling Kindersley titles including *Top 10 Costa Blanca* and *RealCity Barcelona*, as well as guides for other publishers to Crete, Vienna and many other destinations.

The author wishes to thank all in Malta who provided her with invaluable help, among them: Shirley Psaila at the Maltese tourist office; Pierre Cassar at Heritage Malta; Mario Farrugia at Fondazzjoni Wirt Artna; Jo Balzan at St John's Co-Cathedral; Stephen Cini at Gozo's Museum of Archaeology; Tanya van Poucke and her delightful family at Dar ta Zeppi; Freddie at the Animal Sanctuary; and Lucia Mizzi.

Additional contributor
Juliet Rix

Publishing Director Georgina Dee

Publisher Vivien Antwi

Design Director Phil Ormerod

Editorial Sophie Adam, Ankita Awasthi Tröger, Dipika Dasgupta, Rachel Fox, Lucy Richards, Sally Schafer, Jackie Staddon, Hollie Teague

Cover Design Richard Czapnik

Design Tessa Bindloss, Vinita Venugopal

Commissioned Photography Rough Guides / Eddie Gerald, Rough Guides / Victor Borg, Antony Souter

Picture Research Taiyaba Khatoon, Sumita Khatwani, Ellen Root

Cartography Dominic Beddow, Simonetta Giori, Casper Morris, Animesh Pathak

Mapping for Malta and Gozo derived from the Mapping Unit, Malta Environment and Planning Authority (MEPA)

DTP Jason Little

Production Igrain Roberts

Factchecker Toni DeBella

Proofreader Susanne Hillen

Indexer Hilary Bird

Picture Credits

Tony C French 19crb; Heritage Images 12crb, 38b; Martin Novak 97cl; Pacific Press 61clb; Photo 12 17br; Print Collector 95c; Sylvain Sonnet 26br; Sascha Steinbach 40br; Westend61 52clb.

Heritage Malta Head Office: 40tl.

Hotel Juliani: 79b.

iStockphoto.com: Aksenovko 101br; danilovi 22–3; Andrey Danilovich 94c; DavorLovincic 59tr; Deejpilot 4crb; Freeartist 3tr, 106–107; kparis 18br; nejdetduzen 74–5; Neonyn 32–3; Petroos 103tl; Sigarru 60t; SteveAllenPhoto 1.

Malta Aviation Museum: 54cl.

Malta National Aquarium: 55tl.

Mint, Tas-Sliema: 78tl.

Rex Shutterstock: Jane Taylor 25tl; Werner Forman Archive 28cla.

Robert Harding Picture Library: 10cl; Tibor Bognar 6bl; Nick Servian 16br.

SuperStock: age fotostock / Arturo Cano Miño 91cl, / Christian Goupi 69tl, / Nikhilesh Haval 89tl; Hemis.fr / Ludovic Maisant 66clb.

TwentyTwo: 77t.

Cover
Front and spine: **Getty Images:** robertharding
Back: **Dreamstime.com:** Rui G. Santos

Pull Out Map Cover
Getty Images: robertharding

All other images © Dorling Kindersley
For further information see:
www.dkimages.com

Penguin Random House

Printed and bound in China

First American Edition 2007
Published in the US by
DK Publishing, 345 Hudson Street,
New York, New York 10014

Copyright 2007, 2018 © Dorling
Kindersley Limited

A Penguin Random House Company

10 11 20 21 10 9 8 7 6 5 4 3 2 1

Reprinted with revisions 2009, 2011, 2013, 2015, 2018

Published in Great Britain by Dorling Kindersley Limited.

A catalog record for this book is available from the Library of Congress.

ISSN 1479-344X
ISBN 978 1 4654 6906 9

MIX
Paper from responsible sources
FSC™ C018179

SPECIAL EDITIONS OF DK TRAVEL GUIDES

DK Travel Guides can be purchased in bulk quantities at discounted prices for use in promotions or as premiums. We are also able to offer special editions and personalized jackets, corporate imprints, and excerpts from all of our books, tailored specifically to meet your own needs.

To find out more, please contact:

in the US
specialsales@dk.com

in the UK
travelguides@uk.dk.com

in Canada
specialmarkets@dk.com

in Australia
penguincorporatesales@ penguinrandomhouse.com.au

As a guide to abbreviations in visitor information blocks: **Adm** = admission charge; **D** = dinner; **L** = lunch.

Phrase Book

Virtually everyone in Malta is bilingual and speaks Malti and English with equal fluency. Locals don't expect visitors to be able to speak Malti, but appreciate efforts to say a few words in their language. The written Maltese language uses some unsual characters – some letters are crossed and others have a dot. This means that some place names, for example, can be hard to pronounce without a little help.

Maltese Pronunciation Key

ċ - as ch in church	e – as in get
g – (hard) as in good	ġ - (soft) as in gentle
h – usually silent	ħ – as "h" in hand
i – (long) as "ee", e.g. see	j – as "y" in yacht
għ – usually silent	q – silent
x – (soft) as "sh", e.g. sheep	ż - (soft) as in zebra
z – as "ts", e.g. cats	

In an Emergency

Get the police	Sejjaħ pulizija	sey-yah pul-its-iya
Danger	Periklu	peh-ree-klu
Fire	Nar	nahr
Get a doctor	Sejjaħ tabib	sey-yah tab-eeb
Go away	Mur 'l hemm	moor lemm
Help	Ajjut	eye-ut
I'm lost	Intlift	int-lift
Police	Pulizija	poo-lee-tsee-yah

Communication Essentials

Yes	Iva	ee-vah
No	Le	leh
Please	Jekk jogħġbok	yek yoj-bok
Thank you	Grazzi	grah-tsi
very much	ħafna	ha-fnah
You're	M'hemmx	memsh
welcome	mn'hiex	mneesh
Good morning	Bongu	bohn-joo
Good evening	Bonswa	bohn-swar
Good night	Il-lejl it-tajjeb	ill-ale ee-tay-eb
Goodbye	Saħħa	sah-ha
So long	Caw	chow
See you later	Narak iktar tard	nah-rak ik-tah tard
Sorry!	Skużani!	skoo-zah-nee
Where?	Fejn?	fayn
How?	Kif?	keef
When?	Meta?	meh-tah
What?	X'hini?	sheen-eey
Why?	Għaliex?	ah-leesh
Who?	Min?	meen
Which?	Liema?	lee-mah

Useful Phrases

Pleased to	Għandi	ahn-dee pee-yach-eer
meet you	pjacir	
How are you?	Kif inti?	keef een-tee

Very well, thanks	Tajjeb, grazzi	tay-eb, grah-zee
And you?	ħafna U inti?	haf-nah oo een-tee
I beg your pardon?	Skuzi?	skoo-zee
Excuse me	Skuzi!	skoo-zee
Where is…?	Fejn hu…?	fayn oo
Where are…?	Fejn huma?	fayn oo-mah
Where can I find?	Fejn nista insib?	feyn nee-stah een-seeb
How long…?	Kemm iddum?	kehm ee-duhm
How much/many?	Kemm…?	kehm
How much is this?	Kemm iqum dan/din?	kehm ee-um dahn/deen
Do you speak English?	Titkellem bl-Ingliz?	teet-keh-luhm bul een-gleese
I understand	Nifhem	nee-fehm
I don't understand	Ma nifhimx	mah nee-fimsh
Can you help?	Tista' tgħinni?	tis-tah tay-nee
I'd like	Nixtieq	nish-ti
We'd like	Nixtiequ	nish-ti-oo
I'm lost	Intlift	eent-leeft
Happy Christmas!	Il-Milied it-Tajjeb!	eel mee-leed eet-tay-eb
Happy New Year!	Is-Sena t-Tajba!	iss-ehn-nah eet-tay-bah
Happy Easter!	L-Għid it-Tajjeb!	layd eet tay -eb
Best Wishes!	Xewqat Sbieh!	shew-aht sbee
Congratulations!	Nifraħlek!	nee-frah-rah-lek
Good luck!	Ix-Xorti t-Tajba!	ish-shore-tee eet-tay-bah

Numbers

0	xejn	shayn
1	wieħed	wee-het
2	tnejn	tneyn
3	tlieta	tleetah
4	erbgħa	ehr-bah
5	ħamsa	hum-sah
6	sitta	sit-tah
7	sebgħa	seh-bah
8	tmienja	tmeen-yah
9	disgħa	diss-ah
10	għaxra	ahsh-rah
11	ħdax	hdahsh
12	tnax	tnahsh
13	tlettax	tlet-tahsh
14	erbatax	ehr-bah-tahsh
15	ħmistax	hmiss-tahsh
16	sittax	sit-tash
17	sbatax	zbah-tahsh
18	tmintax	tmin-tahsh
19	dsatax	tsa-tahsh

	għoxrin	aw-shreen
	wieħed u	wee-het oo
	għoxrin	aw-shreen
	tnejn u	tneyn oo
	għoxrin	aw-shreen
	tletin	tle-teen
	erbgħin	er-beyn
	ħamsin	hum-seen
	sittin	sit-teen
	sebgħin	se-beyn
	tmenin	tmen-een
	dirgħin	dir-jin
00	mija	mee-yah
,000	elf	elf
,000,000	miljun	mill-yoon

Pronunciation of Place Names

Some places – for example, those with Italian names like Valletta – are pronounced just as they are spelt. But Maltese names can be tongue-twisters for visitors. Here are some of the trickier ones:

Birżebbuġa	beer-zeb-boo-jah
Bugibba	boo-jib-bah
Ċirkewwa	cheer-keh-wah
Dwejra	dway-rah
Ġgantija	ja-gun-tee-yah
Ħaġar Qim	ha-jar-qeem
Ħal Luqa	hull-loo-qah
Ħal Tarxien	hull-tahr-shin
Il-Mellieħa	ill-mell-ee-hah
Il-Qawra	ill-qow-rah
In-Naxxar	In-nahsh-shar
Is-Siggiewi	iss-sidge-ee-wee
Ix-Xagħra	ish-shah-rah
Ix-Xewkija	ish-show-kee-jah
Ix-Xlendi	ish-shlen-dee
L-Għarb	lahrb
L-Imdina	lim-dee-nah
L-Imġarr	lim-jar
L-Imsida	lim-see-dah
Marsaxlokk	marsah-shlock
Paċeville	pah-che-vill

Valletta Street Names

Most street signs are in Malti, but it's worth being familiar with their English equivalents; most shops and businesses use them, some maps are in English only – and you may simply find it easier to say South St than Triq Nofs In-Nħar. Here is a selective list:

Britannja, Triq	Brittania St
Girolamo Cassar, Triq	Girolamo Cassar St
Id-Dejqa, Triq	Strait St
Il-Batterija, Triq	Battery St
Il-Fontana, Triq	Fountain St
Il-Fran, Triq	Old Bakery St
Il Mall	The Mall
Il-Mediterran, Triq	Mediterranean St
Il-Merkanti, Triq	Merchant's St
Il-Punent, Triq	West St
Ir-Repubblika, Misraħ	Republic Sq
Ir-Repubblika, Triq	Republic St
It-Teatru L'Antik, Triq	Old Theatre St
Kastilja, Misraħ	Castille Sq
L-4 Ta' Settembru, Misraħ	4th September Sq
L-Arċisqof, Triq	Archbishop St
L-Assedju L-Kbir, Triq	Great Siege Rd
L'Ispar Il-Quadim, Triq	Old Hospital St
Lascaris, Triq	Lascaris St
L'Imithen, Triq	Windmill St
Marsamxett, Triq	Marsamxett St
Mattia Preti, Pjazza	Mattia Preti Sq
Melita, Triq	Melita St
Nelson, Triq	Nelson St
Nofs In-Nħar, Triq	South St
Papa Benedittu XV, Misraħ	Pope Benedict XV St
Papa Piju V, Triq	Pope Pius V
San Bastian, Triq	St Sebastian St
San Duminku, Triq	St Dominic St
San Ġwann, Misraħ	St John Sq
San Ġwann, Triq	St John St
San Kristofru, Triq	St Christoper St
San Marku, Triq	St Mark St
San Nikola, Triq	St Nicholas St
San Patrizju, Triq	St Patrick St
San Pawl, Triq	St Paul St
Sant' Anna, Triq	St Anna St
Sant' Ursula, Triq	St Ursula St
Santa Lucija, Triq	St Lucija St
Sarria, Triq	Sarria St
Zakkarija, Triq	Zachary St
Zekka, Triq	Old Mint St

Selected Malta and Gozo map index

Valletta sight index

Selected Valletta street index